C000264701

STOP THE STIGMA

-

A PoetsIN Anthology

STOP THE STIGMA

Copyright © 2018 by Poets*IN*

Design by Poets*IN*
Edited by Poets*IN*

poetsin.com

First Edition

CONTENTS

"BUT I BELIEVE"

Moriah

I'll be happy again
Someday
You'll see

I'll live in the meantime
Not live
I'll breathe

I'm broken right now
But there's more
I see

I know it will be mine
It's coming
For me

Or rather
I'm running
One step at a time

Sluggish and slow
But right now
That's fine

Because I see a future
Right ahead of me
Not too far off now

I'll get there, you'll see.

EXISTENTIAL CRISIS

By Peter Hickman

I'm having an existential crisis;
A mental breakdown of sorts
Where I feel completely disconnected
From everything but my obsessive thoughts.
Although all these 'thoughts' seem more like questions
Which are too deep for my mind.
Like why do we tread materially
Through a life that could leave us hanging, blind?

What happens when our journey is over?
Do we simply turn to dust?
In a subjective state of stricken grief
All of these questions become far too much.
For I fear I've opened a gigantic
Evanescent can of worms
Which, given enough time, will disappear
Alongside what my conscious spirits learnt.

AND WHAT THE FUCK IS NORMAL ANYWAY?

Sammie Adams

normal is subjective, surely?
a grey area where none of us
can agree if we're more normal than the
person next door
or our friend
or the stranger doing strange things
on the tube

if normal is when you wake up
at 3am because your duvet isn't equal
on either side of the bed
and you can't sleep when it's like that
so you tiptoe around in the dark
feeling your way
with sleep filled eyes
making sure it is even
before getting back into bed
and sticking your foot out
just to measure it once more,

i am normal.

if normal is avoiding
handles
that are alive with bacteria
that your mind's eye can see
that your lungs can feel

i'm normal.

I'm so normal that I wash my hands
more than the recommended
"After using the toilet"
"After sneezing"
"Before eating"
"After preparing chicken"
Etcetera
I carry antibacterial hand gel
So powerful that if swallowed
You'd get drunk
My sleeves are stretched
From guarding my skin
Against the viruses
On the handrails
On the handles
On the ATM buttons
On the shopping trollies
On anything

I'm normal
I make it my mission to be diligent
-click my car keys three times
-walk away
-click it once more
Four times in total
Because odd numbers
don't feel right;
just like the duvet
everything needs to be even.

I've got a place for almost everything
at home
-I'll know if it's moved by a millimetre
and subconsciously
I'll move it back.

I've an order
A routine
A robotic response to making tea
Washing up
Folding laundry
A process, tried and tested

Why do I do these things?
I have absolutely no idea.
I'm normal, right?
So why question it?
The only thing I ever question;
What the fuck is normal, anyway

I/YOU/HE/SHE/THEY
By Stuart Webb

Who's the one who took my skin
And ran amok whilst dressed akin
Doused in darkness dappled down
Flooded the circus with tears of clown

Who's the one who took my face
And lost his leg of the human race
Who inspired insipid indulgent tears
And gave free rein to abstract fears

Who took the keys and drove my soul
Across keyboards to the Facebook cull
Who severed the server and outside lines
And stored his humour in rancid brine

I'm the one who wakes up cold
To mosaic messages to only be told
"Where were you? Although you were there
Those bags, your eyes in shades of despair"

We're the ones stood in the absent light
Who accept the bark and regret the bite
With our sense of self on a rolling boil
And barbed anxiety in tight wound coil

You're the one who knows what I mean
Trapped between the cracks in your dreams
You're the one who can climb out too
Keep on keeping on, keep on being you

I AIM TO PLEASE

By Leah Beckstrom

"Every action comes with a consequence. Either positive or negative, a consequence always occurs. I knew that when I accepted this gift, I knew I'd be in for it pretty rough." He paced around his cluttered apartment, muttering to himself like a madman. Something he does often of late.

"Probably some crazy side effect of my—" The man's eyes alone portrayed a never-ending civil war inside his mind. He continued speaking to his imaginary audience.

"Others blindly assume it is a gift. Or should I say punishment? Let's call it a punishment." He shook his finger in content of the word.

"One that I'm not sure I deserve for all that I do."

The man took a few steps forward and held his hand out in front of him, mocking the pose of a host.

"Yes, you in the back. What's your question? What is it exactly that I do? Good question, sir. Very good."

A malicious-looking grin crept onto his five o'clock shadow, and he shook his head in disgust of the action.

"Well, I'm glad you asked. I basically just have to point at someone and they magically become happy."

The deep, throaty chuckle was agonizing even to his own ears. Other than the remains of phlegm in his throat, the suite was silent.

"All right, settle down. I know it's crazy. Don't even ask me how the science works because I don't fucking know." His hand shot up to cover his mouth.

"Excuse my language; that's very unprofessional of me. As you can see," He laughed deliriously again for a moment, settling into a lack of air and a coughing fit, "I am quite riled up by this new lifestyle I have adopted."

The man tossed his invisible microphone back and forth between his calloused hands and could almost feel the weight of it pulling him faster than his insanity.

"You might say I brought this on myself. I could have rejected this odd offer. But—" He put one finger up to silence the non-existent stadium. Swivelling his head frequently around him several times, he was satisfied.

"At the time of the offer, I believe—correct me if I'm wrong—but, I believe that I was willing to do whatever it took to help others. I know, right? Ludicrous. It's ludicrous, I tell you!"

He scanned the crowd and landed next to the fridge where he saw his target.

"Oh, man. Someone piss in your cereal this morning?" The grin started to creep back again.

"Or do you just dislike my sense of humor? I know something that will cheer you up." He spun around dramatically and pointed in the direction of the fed-up figment.

"Look at that cheeky smile, you! You're happy, and those around you are too! But honestly, I don't give two shits. Because you know what?" The man rested his hands on his knees as he appeared to close in on the imaginary audience member by the fridge.

"Nothing makes me happy anymore!" He shot up quick and paced with more vexation, stomping bare feet along the living room rug as harsh as hail on the East Coast.

"I do all this for you! And I receive nothing in return because no one can know it's me." He emphasized every word. "No one will ever know it's me."

"Maybe that's the science of this outrageous curse. Maybe the fact that not one single person will ever thank me is what forces me further into depression. One might assume that someone so involved in the world—someone making such a positive contribution—would be at least neutral in their emotional state.

"But no! Not for me! Nothing is ever for me!" He could feel the sweat dripping down his scalding hot cheeks as his eternal rage rose again.

"Believe me, I wish I could feel the way I am supposed to, but it just won't happen."

He took a deep breath and continued once again, this time to finish.

"I guess you could say I aim to please."

This piece is meant to symbolize someone who anxiously and compulsively tries to please everyone around them at the expense of their own happiness, resulting in anger and resentment towards the way they are.

TEMPEST

Beth Lunney

Trying to breathe
through a kaleidoscope
Colored patterns, cascading fears

Swirled dreams, unwanted truths
I stood and faced the gales
Thoughts, conscience
Clarity, unconfined

Cope, push
Silent steps
Re-root

SLEEPING BEAUTY

By Sue & Jo Clennell

Which witch made me sleep?
Who highlighted the kinks of the subconscious?
Of course, sleeping makes me low fuss.
No need to think, I am comforted
by ghosts of the past.
I've had my share of princes.
They say not to go out with men
who ride motorbikes or white vans,
and I've been out with both.
What I need is a shield sister
to accompany me through the mazes,
the land mines of regret, remove the thorns,
help me sow the seeds of wellness.

RISE

By Rich Withey

Life embroidered a heart on my sleeve
Offered it up for the whole world to see
Occasionally something snags at that thread
Perhaps it is something someone did or said
The actions and intentions of spite and jealousy
Perhaps the frustrations of my own inadequacies
Whatever it is that attempts to put holes in your sails
Even your own negative thoughts when positivity fails
It is temporary…

I try to focus on the positives in my darkened days
I think on how I've been blessed in so many ways
I've always been able to gain some form of perspective
Some form of constructive directive
But there have been times where I have stumbled
Where I have lost my way and fell
Sometimes it's hard to recognise your own heaven
While you're crawling through your own personal hell
I have suffered losses by death and tragedy
And I've put some of my own hurt on me
I've thought about abandoning it all
There have been times when I can't see beyond that wall
Your own war fought on grey beaches
Where positivity seldom reaches
Until you give it the space
Allow yourself some time and grace

I guess tragedy has made me stronger
Made me want to wage this war with life longer
Because it's all we got until it's gone
The threat of death should be reason enough to say strong
From the times where I have descended on some sort of debilitating
low
A horrible place where only anxiety has the fuel to grow
Where the lucid parts unravel and I feel the stitches break
Only to come back stronger and fix the mistakes

The ink at night has offered me solutions
It brings a calm to many of my revolutions
I find the dark, the moon and stars have often given me peace
Some form of cathartic and ethereal release
By pouring out my heart on to unbiased pages
It has saved me from many unnecessary cages
It has given me clarity and a resolute will to rise
and taught me a finger to the world is sometimes rather wise…

MELANCHOLIA
By Hannah Fields

Some days, the air feels too heavy to
breathe and the act of living feels like
a meaningless chore—mere busywork
enacted upon my being by the universe.

Still, I rise like a drunken tightrope walker
aimlessly navigating a thin string stretched
between the winter-cracked hands of time
twitching at the impulse of letting go.

The sky is dark, but my eyes are wide
searching for trickles of light between
heartaches laying waste to my soul
beneath this fortress of skin and bone.

I load rose blossoms like bullets into an
imaginary gun meant to clear my mind
but my fingers always catch on thorns
before I can mimic pulling the trigger.

Caught on the cusp of beginning and end
I attempt to rewrite my story on crumpled
ink-soaked pages, though my resurrection
was overwritten some many years ago.

STOIC.

Jack Leibur

I have fear. I have guilt. I have moles on my back that somebody once traced with their fingers and debts that can't be settled.

I'm clumsy with my hands and sensitive. Way too sensitive. And I'm sorry I don't have the stoic shell you wish I had when the tears started to bruise. And all I do is miss me who breaks. Me who burns.

Punch. Wall. Punch. Wall. Red. Red. Red.

And I keep on missing and missing, and I'm so fucking sorry for being such a hungry, empty creature. And there I go with my lack of stoicism again, and I'm just sorry.

And the cold—the cold—the hairs on my arm stand on-end like needles, and suddenly all I see is this mirror I want to smash with my fist and the obnoxious sobbing. The pathetic sobbing that ran out of my mouth like the roadrunner, when I just wanted my throat to get shut. My vocal cords cut off like that episode of The Twilight Zone where the guy lives in a little glass box.

Because isolation is the only cure when I'm like this. Because I'm a shattered vase or a mug with the ear broken, and no.

No.

No. I never meant to leave you.

And I swear, I know how it feels, like a rock tied to your feet when you're alone and abandoned, while I only look for a shred of sincerity in the salt in the wound.

CAN'T YOU

Abbie Dixon

Can't you see the sadness
Behind these laughing lines
Can't you see the madness
Deep inside my eyes

Can't you hear me shouting
Behind the words I'm fine
Can't you hear me screaming
From deep within my mind

Can't you see I'm fighting
To free me from this life
Can't you see I'm hiding
From the mercy of the knife

Can't you tell I'm dying
From deep within my soul
Can't you tell I'm grieving
For a love that can't be told

Can't you see the truth
Behind this life of lies
Can't you see its fantasy
From the truth you must be blind

UNTITLED

Norman Wm. Muise

loneliness
in the pond
 a wet moon

.

"PINNED"

Lynne Shayko

I feel cornered.
You drive stakes about me.
Each one is labelled.

First "bipolar" is driven in the ground.
I am stunned;
it almost pierced me as
you threw it before me,
driving it deep into the earth.

Its language is strange to me,
though I listen carefully
and try to discern its import.

While I try to understand it,
another spear is flung, plunging
into welcoming earth behind me.

I whip about:
borderline personality disorder
is its name.
It speaks a language even stranger
than the first.
I look up to you to interpret,
but your light blinds me and
I cannot see.

Why so bright a light?
To examine me?

Humble me?
Or stun me?

You have succeeded in all three.
You have succeeded.
You may remove your spotlight.

You silently concede and oblige.

But perhaps this is worse.
I am no longer quivering in the light
but in the dark shadows.
I think I hear new stakes falling about me.

It's too dark to see them
or read their names,
but sometimes, late at night,
they whisper to me:
schizoaffective disorder
post-traumatic stress disorder
dissociative identity disorder
paranoia
psychosis
neurosis

I jolt awake
and jump to my feet,
but suddenly it's silent again.
I don't know if I dreamed the words
or truly heard them.

Or maybe I misheard?
Where is my interpreter?

BOUND

By Lucy Slessor

Twisted, binding, self-inflicted
To this pain become addicted
Body burning, mind undone
Scream inside and wish to run

See them wander, see them moan
Spoilt and mindless, all alone
You think it's hard and think it's cruel
Bitter hearts to feed the fuel

They could not, would not want to care
To them their life is so unfair
Wanting more, but not the work
The perks they crave, the effort shirked

Try to moan when faced with pain
Body breaking, mind insane
Try to find some hope inside
It turns you into the battered bride.

DAMAGED LINES
(A VILLANELLE)

By Miriam Ruff

With broken thoughts the mind does go,
Intrepid sailor lost at sea;
Fight to hold the memories you know.

Possession does not make the wanting so,
Strength of self will show you who you need to be;
With broken thoughts the mind does go.

In wispy trails knowledge will yet flow,
Away from port, like pirates will it flee;
Fight to hold the memories you know.

With fear of loss we'll never show,
How ephemeral the mind we cannot see;
With broken thoughts the mind does go.

Troubled is the one who does not know,
That damaged lines will never set you free;
Fight to hold the memories you know,

Steel yourself as winds around you blow,
Waves of remembrances to sea;
With broken thoughts the mind does go,
Fight to hold the memories you know.

(c) 2017 Miriam Ruff

BLACK DOG DOWN.

Paul Chambers

Climbing into flimsy skin
husks of last night's dreams,
focus easily turns its eye
upon grime of the day
and dark facets of life
stink of unwanted touch
fingering conscious hours
in this physical plane.
I say no. No negative.
Not this time.
Find sunshine,
some shine.
See how much good
there always is.
Hold that black dog at bay.
I have this bed, my sturdy roof.
This dry life peppered with foods
and drizzled in water.
Bejewelled with friends.
Feast of family.
I am King,
not a pauper.
I am loved.
And I love.

PERSONALITY

Squeakypeewee01

Dear Personality,

I find you quite fascinating, and I felt a letter to you would help me to understand who and what you really are.

I know that you make me anti-social, paranoid, and lacking of empathy, but why? Did you mean to be this way? Or were my childhood experiences part of this evolution?

I'm not mad at you, but I'm confused to hell. All I ever wanted was a peaceful, normal life, but thanks to you, I have quite the opposite.

There are times that I think a lobotomy would be a really good idea; it would save me a great deal of unwanted emotional pain. But then, I wouldn't be me, would I?

When you were first revealed to me as being something more than just an unwanted shadow, I was terrified, scared that we could never live together. I'm still not entirely sure we can co-exist safely, but at least we are both giving it a go, and for that, I am extremely grateful.

It's strange how life throws so many different curve balls at us. People are hard to read. No thanks to you, I find it even harder than most. Yes, I know that sounds angry and mean, I mean it to be. We can eventually live in peace and harmony, but that doesn't mean I have to like it.

We have some serious challenges ahead, and I hope you'll be by my side rather than stalking my back like a waiting tiger who is far too hungry for its own good.

I will never underestimate the power that you can hold over me, but know this Mister: I am just as strong-willed. You are not the only part of my psyche that functions. I am in control of this vehicle, and the wheel is gripped tightly.

Dual control is not an option here. You are now demoted to second in command. However, this is a privilege I offer, and it can and will be removed at my pleasure.

Don't fuck me about. My personality is growing and changing, which means this 'disorder' is going to be put in order. This will be done by me and you.

I am beginning to love who I am, and this newfound confidence I have is wonderful.

This is all for now but don't forget—we are always going to be together, but only one of us can be in charge. I won't let you keep me in this hell-hole for longer than I need to be. It's time I got you sorted so I can finally go home and be safe.

Yours Sincerely,

Girl X.

DOUBLE DOG DARE YA

Outspoken St. Monk

Now
I open
in this moment
myself to bare
calling
from the well
echoes I hear
myself
in this moment
I open
to the sound
of a thousand swans
crying death
now I open
myself to bare
to quiet my screams
to hug my demons
to love myself
in this moment,

my heartfelt dare

"LATE NIGHT FLEETING SNATCHES"
Moriah

i need to stop melting
into hopelessness and misery and self-destruction and i-give-up
for my family and friends to sweep off the ground
into a dustpan
and pour me back into myself
only to shatter
and melt again

WHEN PANIC COMES KNOCKIN'

By Elisha Clugston

Knock. Knock. Knock.
This beating in my chest
It must be you again
My most unwanted guest
Breathing becomes labored
As I try shutting the door
Begging - pleading
Though I know you'll ignore

Knock. Knock. Knock.
Knees begin to grow weak
I can't beg anymore
I've no tongue left to speak
Worry becomes panic
Immobilized by the fear
Demons and death
Begin to ring in my ear
Knock, knock, knock,
My lungs screaming for air
They're demanding I breathe
But my brain's unaware
All cognitive functions
Begin to quickly shut down
Mind and body
Become panic's playground

Knock, knock, knock,
The door opens to Hell
Though I'm still here on earth

I can feel the heat swell
Now violently shaking
My muscles can't take the pain
Searing voltage
Runs through every membrane

Knock. Knock. Knock.
A pounding in my head
Gates of Hell have been closed
Can't believe I'm not dead
You have gone from me now
But you left wreckage behind
Broken - shattered
Both my body and mind

PLASTIC FLOWERS

Lucian Smith
AGED 12

My wrists feel like a forever sweater
The sleeves, stained with snot
All my life and emotion
Used up for naught
Each night lost
From the false senses
Of life, I once sought

Through the meadows of daisies
Withered from the cold
- the fake smile
I always had to mold
I cried and cried
From the lies I had been told

My body and mind
Finally gave up
And went
Two-fold.

PHANTASM

By Hannah Fields

When I'm alone with myself
all my demons come creeping

from their dark hiding places
tucked at the back of my mind

forcing me to look them in the
eyes while I attempt to sustain

my composure all the while knowing
I'm on the edge of tears that bubble

up beneath my breast in the midnight
hours like the nightmares from my

youth. Although this time no one
comes running to ease the clattering

of my heart as I pull damp sheets
overhead shielding myself from

the anxieties that pull at my feet
with scaled crooked hands.

BETWEEN HEART AND MIND
By Gauranshi Tripathi

The most chilling horror stories do not end with blood and gore; they begin somewhere on the mangled road between the heart and the mind. It's a maze and you are screaming, just not the way victims at the end of the axe murderers' hunt do.

This screaming begins in the hollow and noisy corners of the mind. You hear the echoes and the noises, and it dulls the chasm between reality and imagination.

What if I'm really going mad? Or is it me being lazy and thinking too much? What if these demons that sit on the empty, rattling shelves of my mind never leave, but the people around do? What if I become who I dread, and what I dread is all that's left of me?

Depression doesn't come cloaked in tears and theatrics. It comes at a time when you least expect and paralyses the very sense of well-being. You lose your grounding, and you lose who you are.

What if it doesn't end? What if I'm mad? There could be so many reasons it happened to you, ranging from a love gone bad, to a job, to a family dispute. Getting help doesn't exactly come easy. It costs money and loads of it. What's the point if you sit inside a room and all you can think is, they don't want to hear me talk; they are doing it for the money.

All I can say is it does end. Not today, not tomorrow, but eventually.

While you are fighting it, you're not alone, and the fight doesn't end overnight. It ends just like the discovery, one fine day when you least expect it.

ECLIPSED

By Sue & Jo Clennell

Wrestling the storm,
holding your head above water,
tomorrow is overlooked.
Mind squeezed,
no one is weaving you into
the grand design.

Lined up for no reason,
you look for friends among
the interrogators,
the controllers.

Previously published by Windmills, an Australian zine.

I AM A ROSE

By Helen Smith

I am a rose with no petals
No beautiful scent, no colourful bloom
Only thorns and I
Scratch myself raw.

REQUISITE

By Mark Olmsted

Because some days,
a poem is required.
Some days,
one's marrow
bursts from the seams.
One's vessels, running
neither straight nor narrow,
demand passage through the bone –
like pitchfork-wielding peasants,
marching to torch their own homes.
Some days,
words will out
like rain from a spout,
drenching a parched heart
with blood-wet art.

Some poems
do not believe
in live and let live.
They will make demands,
take as well as give.
These poems
are not afraid to bully,
to slap you awake
from the slumber of
complacency.
There has been far too much lulling going on,
after all.

Some nights,
a poem will be summoned.
Like a gallant lover
wanted less from desire,
than for the cover
of his cape.
The world is round
but its corners are sharp.
Barbed wire punctures
at every juncture,
as you realize with
unbounded grief,
that you are complicit
in its manufacture.

So today I will make
your poem,
and long for the day
when it is a gift,
instead of a necessity.

THE CARTOGRAPHER

Leanne Moden

I wear this map to show where I have been;
its pathways raised like secret lines of Braille.
The contours are inscribed upon my skin
to represent the mountains I have scaled.

Some stretches of the surface look like lace
or snakeskin, spreading down across my spine.
And now I'm old, there is no inch of space
not covered by these overlapping lines.

It's ten years since I added to my map,
and though sometimes I feel directionless,
no longer is my body like a trap;
no longer do I bleed when under stress.

This map may show the mountains I have crossed,
but now I know I'm better found than lost.

First published in 'Madder than we look' Edited by Hayley Green (Big White Shed: 2016)

THIRTEEN

Melodic Rose

Thirteen,
Bells toll at the stroke of midnight
One for each flame burning on the candle of youth
One for each smile sloping at the setting of the sun
One for each simmering heartbeat
Losing its pace.

Thirteen,
One number for each dream
Carefully falling into the northern sea
A current picks up the pieces now
Scatters it to the wind
Leaving behind nothing
But thirteen.

Thirteen,
Bare bones crossed
In the empty roadside shack
Oil stove leaks into the great river
Floating down the bay
Leaving nothing behind
No memories
No thoughts
Just a dream that says,

You were never needed here, thirteen.

So you wrote a pact today.
Wrote your name in blood, thirteen.
Simply said, tomorrow we die by fire
Or we keep trying.

Simply said, goodnight to the orange hue
Of indifference in the sky above.

Tearing your life away from the
Sparseness of a town that held nothing for you.

How did we not know about you, Thirteen?
How did we claim your silence
When every moment
Every day
Your silence was screaming out for attention?
Why did we bring flowers to your door,
Thirteen
On the day we realized that you could be
Would be no more?

They say they have foiled you
Taken the knitting needles
From out of the powdered smoke
The long arms that you keep hidden out of sight.

Thirteen,
You cannot imagine
How much my heart
Has fallen at your feet
Compassion for the road your feet have tread
And I know it all too well.

What was it that caused the wolves
To swell up and meet you
Licking the base of your feet?

And when you ran did you
Feel the heat of fire scorch your belly
In the night?

Thirteen,
The dogs are chasing you
Grabbing onto the collar of your old
Jacket
Only dark skin
Tan skinned feels the same
In the middle of winter.

They say there are multiples of you
That thirteen was really just the remnant
Of the hundred.

One hundred bolts of iron
That streaked down
From the sky
Hitting the clock every time.

I know your story, thirteen,
For yours and mine
Are one in the same.

We are warriors after all.

Tall beings who stood in the face
Of clenched teeth and snarling jaws

And would not lie down in fear.

I know the feeling of a panic after midnight
How heavy the world can seem
When ice has crawled around the base of your neck
Filling your veins to frozen.

Perhaps there's no catcher for the heart of you
But we were all taken
Vanished into the cusp of a world
That forgot to honour our contributions.

They built fortresses of hopelessness
Across our memories
Telling us to bring our children to the well
For sacrifice.

Only you forgot not to listen.
We all did and should have been listening to you instead.

Your voices have mingled in between the gusts
Of April snow.

Whisper Attawapiskat.

Tell us your stories and your scars
Tell us your sorrows and your triumph
Over the hand of the dark
Attempting to clutch one life out
Of existence and send sprawling into the black.

Tell us your pact.

The one driven by your need to be remembered
Or not remembered at all
Because no one should ever be made
To feel as if they don't have a choice
No life should ever be left
Dancing in the ground.

No child should ever have to pick out
Their casket like a limo
And their funeral suit
Like a dress to the prom.

Thirteen,
Dancing on the doors of Attawapiskat
On behalf of every single soul
Who turned their eyes down to the ground
And claimed that your story was not
Really important enough to be told.

Who shoved your lives into the forbidden
Isolated coven.

I am sorry.
I am sorry.
I am.

We are all here.
And you should be too.

**Note

On April 12, 2016, the Canadian village of Attawapiskat was struck by tragedy when 13 Aboriginal youths made a suicide pact.

The youngest was just 9 years old.

It was not long before this story made national headlines across Canada, even reaching the federal government, and within days, therapists and other mental health workers started to pour into this community in order to intervene.

Decades of poverty, ostracization, and a lack of government funding for basic living conditions has led to an onslaught of alcoholism, substance abuse, and other forms of mental illness within the Aboriginal community.

What happened at Attawapiskat was not only a tragedy, but a wake-up call.

As a young woman who is considered a minority, I am all too familiar with the effects trauma can have on someone's mental health.

When we speak of treating someone for depression, suicide, anxiety, substance abuse, one must also look at the conditions in which these individuals have lived.

It is true that mental health is oftentimes a result of a genetic disposition, and it is very possible for the child of someone who has experienced trauma to also feel the effects of that trauma, even though they may be a generation removed from the actual events.

When you factor in centuries of colonialism, genocide, bigotry, poverty, and the fact that even in 2017, a person can still be hated for the colour of their skin, can still be despised for the genitalia they carry between their legs, or denied access to a job just because of their religion and language, it is not hard to see that the burden of such a history can carry the deepest of wounds; a scar that, although invisible, is still undeniably powerful.

For anyone who has ever lived on the fringes and felt the hand of erasure, I hope that my words will speak to you in some tangible way.

For the people of Attawapiskat, I honour you with this poem.

ALL IT NEEDS IS A KISS OF SWEET AIR

By Sarala Ram Kamal

Writhed in nightmares
Taut nerves
Lurking fear
Pounding anxiety

Brain's soil lost fertility
Famine struts through dark moments
Fear gnaws at the husk of thoughts

Violent flights
Curdled blood
Crouched in damp corners

Faces dark with bloody tongues
Hands with long sharp nails
Death in different masks

Want of ending
Ending of agony

Languid moods
Sluggish with dank guts

Knots in thoughts
Illusions

Not the callous indifference
All it needs is a kiss of sweet air
All it needs is a kiss of sweet air
All it needs is a kiss of sweet air

WE, INVISIBLE

by Norbert Gora

looking at the smile
that covers the face
you just can't see
the boiling lake of pain
it chokes the soul
like a suicide rope
it drains the mind
of joy and hope

glancing into the eyes
you don't notice
the creeping shadows of anxiety
squeezing through the veins
with blood

maybe a man next door
calls for relief in suffering
but the glass wall of your ignorance
drowns every word born of despair

we, invisible
weakened by the demons of daily hardship
we walk along
the soulless streets

they, unaware
throw out the sentences
that hurt more than a long knife
fumes of sneer settle on our naked necks

SCREAMING ON THE INSIDE

By Peter Hickman

I am screaming on the inside
All this is hidden from my brain.
I'm pathetic, even stupid;
I am going totally insane.
I am holding onto anguish,
Projecting onto others my fears;
I'm too scared to take a journey
Without the help given by my peers.

I am screaming on the inside;
The laughter's gone and has long since died.
I'm right back to the beginning
Of what is an emotional ride.
I am breathing only bad times;
It's an air so dark and thick you choke.
I no longer hold onto dreams,
As others have all gone up in smoke.

I am screaming on the inside;
I have felt like this for a long while;
Life is never ending torment
So my blood's now running down this tile.
I was looking for an answer,
But I realised there is no hope.
So my future's back in my hands,
As long as I let go of the rope.

CATATONIA

By Carol Alena Aronoff

She had managed to fly to London
clutching R.D. Laing's, "Knots,"
her last hope. Her world had been
reduced to black and white, confined
to two dimensions. Body rigid, her skin
prickled with fear. She was a petrified forest.

Still as a statue, she stood in the corner
of her bare room for hours facing the wall
or curled into crash pose, arms bracing
thighs, head touching knees, eyes
shutting the world out. No words
for the hell realm she inhabited.

When the ice of her terror melted
just a little, she let me sit beside her.
It took weeks for her to look at me,
longer for her to speak in little more
than a slight breeze. I had to move
closer to listen, had to remain still.

She told me she couldn't hear me
because she wasn't really there.
Not knowing how to answer, I told her
I loved her. I said that she was safe.
Some days, she let me hold her
for hours until she could finally uncurl.

She called me the Angel from the Void.

A BRIGHTER FLAME

By Rich Withey

I poured the ink
I let it flow
Cascading like midnight
The release I know
Darkened locks
Drowned my face
But I took a deep breath
Exploded into space
Delicately
I paint my face
Emerald eyes stare
Through a mascara glare
Sanguine taste on my lips
Delicate breath at your hips
Purple and black essence
From the bottle to the pout
I whisper on the candles
They return a shout
A brighter flame
More insane
While I play the freak
I dance and flail
I incite hail
Your lipstick on my cheek
The dark is my reflection
It savours my complexion
It takes me deep within
When the lights are on
The night reflects my song

Gloss and shine
Bound with PVC
Failed psychotherapy
As nets ensnare my frame
I quietly reclaim...

Me

"SECRETS IN THE CLOSET"

By: Nancy Xiong

It's cold and dark. That's how I like it here in the closet where I hide. She is my refuge. She is my friend.

I hide from everyone: my husband, my siblings, my parents, my friends. Sometimes, I even hide from God.

I hide because everyone is oblivious to my presence, to my pain. I hide because everyone chooses to ignore my circumstances. I hide because everyone runs away from helping me carry the load of my disease.

I hide when I am alone. I hide because I am alone.

I hide when I cannot draw the pain out as it runs deep within my veins--in my blood, flowing to the tips of my being, so that I ache everywhere. I want to draw out the pain. I need to draw out the pain, the pain in my blood.

I cut it out with a steel blade, here in the closet. I cut it out with a safety pin, here in the closet. I cut it out with my fingernails, here in the closet. I cut it out.
In the closet, the air is stuffy and cold, and I like it. It runs over my body and it cools me, it soothes me. Like a lullaby, it sings over the raging fire of the beast and she falls asleep.

I lay here, in the closet. I lay very still in the closet. I fall asleep in the closet. And the closet keeps my secrets.

BLACKOUT
(A RONDEAU REDOUBLÉ)

By Miriam Ruff

Descending into darkness makes me strong
The fear and anger put me in the fray
Once there, the time I spend will oft be long
The flames of rage don't see the light of day

I revel in the darkness, there I stay
And unconcerned if it be right or wrong
The horrors of the mind show me the way
Descending into darkness makes me strong

As I dig in, I bring the hate along
Self-loathing guides my step, won't let me stray
It's ringing like the striking of a gong
The fear and anger put me in the fray

Resistance not an option, I say nay
Within the darkness is where I belong
My soul shows monsters all out on display
Once here, the time I spend will oft be long

The struggle with the demons is lifelong
The fight with hatred always on replay
In darkness my heart truly sings its song
The flames of rage don't see the light of day

I revel in the blackness, come what may
Where days are short and nights are always long
From my true path I cannot move away
The fear and anger make me so headstrong
Descending into darkness

(c) 2017 Miriam Ruff

BROKEN

Soulhearts

we are all broken
torn pieces of faded fabric
all frayed at the edges

flapping in the wind
hanging on to a rusty clothesline
drying under the sun

we are all part of a pattern
in a loom that never
ceases to sew

interwoven threads
composed of you and i
in different colored hues

NO ONE IS NORMAL

Cardinal Cox

Your teachers at school
Had secrets they wouldn't
Want to share out loud
They weren't normal

The policeman who drinks
A little too much to relax
Before arresting himself to bed
He's not normal

The doctors who worry
That they made the right
Diagnosis in the surgery
They aren't normal

The neighbours who never
Meet your gaze in
The street outside your home
They aren't normal

Politicians shouting at each other
Every single night
On the haunted box
They aren't normal

All those folks crammed
Into the tube just to
Get to their hated work
They aren't normal

Pop-stars appearing in every newspaper
Trying to tempt you
To buy their latest tune
They aren't normal

Whole villages, whole towns
Whole tower blocks, whole cities
Screaming with their fears
They aren't normal

So if none of us are normal
It must be normal for
All of us not to be normal
Especially me

EAGLES

Vibha Lohani

Claws
impale
the flesh
of my being

Aerie
flutters
chaos
in my
mind

Beaks
dig
into the
soul

Blood
scatters
across
deserted
heart

Wings
blow
me away...
helter-skelter

Crimson
spurts
drench
my body

Lips
cracked
dry

Parched
voice
stifled
by
ash grey
feathers

Delusions
they say
inside
my head
Eagles
say I …

'MEMOIRS OF A MOTH'

Firdaus Parvez

I'm a moth, dull and ugly.

My wings have grown inwards. My shoulder blades itch to burst them out. People find me strange or, rather, confusing. I'm just an ugly moth, a little confused myself.

When I was little, I loved books and sharp pencils. The latter, because I liked to sketch birds and butterflies.

I never used pencil sharpeners; I would 'borrow' blades from my father's shaving kit then would snap them through the middle, hiding one half inside my pillow cover.

Slicing through the wood and graphite was intriguing. Carving out a point on the pencil was fun. Most of the time, I would cut my fingertips, sometimes quite deep. The pain kept me up at night for hours.

Once, I experimented on my wrist.

My parents went crazy when they saw the blood. I couldn't understand their concern. It was just a cut.

My mother cried for days, and I was taken to a therapist, who confused me even further.

I remember the first time I saw her. That strange girl who looked familiar, yet someone I'd never seen before. I remember that day because it was a day after my sixteenth birthday.

Grandma had been ill for a while, and my mother wanted to visit her on the weekend. We had been on the road for a few hours, and I was getting restless. I had fought with my boyfriend, and it was playing on my mind. I was being the classic rebellious teenager, and I could sense my mother holding her temper. It was a bad day.

Grandma's house was a double storied one. I was given a room on the top floor; it had a large window overlooking the garden. It used to be my mother's room when she lived here.

There was a full-length mirror, with a beautiful wooden frame on one wall. I had walked to it after unpacking, and that's when I saw her.

She was beautiful in a strange way.

Her curly black hair hung past her shoulders, glossy and thick. It made me conscious about my thinning curls.

She had large eyes, slightly popping, like a butterfly's: dark-brown luminous honey-drops.

She was looking at me like she knew me, yet not. I tried to smile; she gave me a nervous smile too. A dimple danced on her left cheek. I had a little dent on my right one, I remembered.

We stepped closer, and I reached out to her. She did, too, till our fingertips touched.

Her wrist was smooth, no scars like my ugly one. Her skin was soft brown, mine dull silvery of moth dust.

I watched her cobalt wings unfurl behind her.

She's a butterfly, I gasped.

It was surreal. We stood there looking at each other for a long time.

She was gone as suddenly as she had appeared. My wrist dripped the sadness I felt: a dark red streak on the mirror. I sobbed at the loss.

I took a long hot shower, washing away my grief, the hot water hurting my wrist as I watched the blood swirl down the drain.

That is when I felt the pain in my shoulder blades. My wings burst out. They hung limp behind me like old rags. I had to get out; the steam from the shower was suffocating me.

I threw open the window and climbed onto the ledge.

Water dripped down my naked body, and the cold breeze almost knocked me down.

I felt a presence beside me. It was her, dripping wet, standing on the ledge with me. Her wings were gone; just scars remained where they once were.

I felt my wings unfurl. I flapped them dry. They were cobalt blue.

She had given me her wings.

I looked at her, my eyes swimming. She smiled; I smiled back.

"Time to fly," we whispered together.

My toes nervously curled around the edge of the ledge. I took a deep breath...

Later, I learned that a moth can't fly with butterfly wings.

MOVING FORWARD...

Jessica Macaluso

"It's okay," I tried to reassure her
"I will bring you with me
We can both move forward
We can both succeed"
She won't agree
She is stubborn and mean
She's hurt
So deeply wounded
Sometimes she doesn't trust me
Me! Me, who carries her around
Me, who allows her to throw her fits
When she gets upset
I suppose her fears are real
If we move forward
If we succeed
She will dwindle away
And die

"THESE SCORES"

Moriah

These scores
On flesh
Tell broken things

They speak
Of blade
The pain it brings

Laments
The loss
Of whole fresh skin

The breaks
Bleed out
The pain within.

The pain
Wells out
With scarlet drops

It beads
And runs
And finally stops

It's wiped
Away
Fresh scores to heal

The raw
Pink flesh
You love to feel

Some days
Soon pass
And tears do close

The fine
White lines
Behind are those

These scores
They scream
Of cries for peace

These scores
They tell
Of pain released.

DROWNING

Rowane S Carberry

Trapped inside the flames of my own living hell
With claws of despair ripping at my throat
Searching for anything to keep me afloat
While seeds of depression settle in and swell

Inside a mind that is chaotic and dark
Inside a mind that can't see the truth anymore
With eyes that look at a reflection they abhor
They see a personality that has lost its spark

Lungs being flooded with the shadows of isolation
Whilst I stand surrounded in a crowd but still separate and alone
Imagining what it would be like to stand staring at my headstone
Knowing that death would be better than living this eternal damnation

A body and mind crippled and in pain
With scars that won't fade
Sick of pretending and playing in this charade
So I go out dancing and drown myself in the rain.

© Rowanne S Carberry 25/04/16

THE END

Sharmila Mitra

Scudding clouds across a violent sky
are my feelings gone weird and awry
after a lifetime
of middle-class compromise over every single thing.

The first starlight that might have touched me
and made a star on my baby's forehead
never arrived
though I was born on a clear, star-studded night.

Saturday's child, and a girl, and no silver spoon
still, I have travelled the dusty road
and drank
the stale wine of left-over joy.

Childhood, youth flew by on a seagull's wings
the wind screaming, which I thought was my own screaming
but no
decent people do not scream
or tear their hair or cry hot tears.

They wait and wait and wait and wait
for the Fates to train their attention on them
so did I
waited for the windfall that was going to be the wind under my wings
helping me fly, soar to the sky.

In the fifth decade of my life, I think
that I have had a stand on the brink

of the adventure
that was never to be.

But at least the awakening in me
of a stargazer's soul has a nightly engagement
rising above the estrangement of the world, and the void
that used to engulf me, as a Black Hole swallows a star.

I swear, I will not end with a whimper but a big bang
My memory
May not be
What you would
Want to see

But I shall rise to the horizon.

I shall be a supernova
a catastrophic explosion of heat
energy, colours
and a scattering of waves
a titanic self-immersion.

WALK INTO SUNSHINE

Shakunthala Preeth

Mystical aura crimson hue
Filling the dreams with subtle cue

Wake up my friend, open your eyes
Look deep within for hows and whys

Go beyond all the qualms and lies
To the realm of eternal ties
Among the stars and endless skies
Seek and do what your heart complies

Gather your grit and follow through
The spirit knows where to take you

© *Shakunthala Preeth* | *2017*

AN ODE TO MENTAL ILLNESS.

Sammie Adams

i know you think
i am the cliche,
the woman who wears
her heart on her sleeve
and i know
because i flash the flesh
of my aorta
from underneath
my jumper
you thought you
could take advantage
of my oversized ventricles
without my eyes seeing
what my heart didn't want to feel

i noticed your falsehoods
i saw the things you wanted to hide
beneath extra layers of skin
wrapped up tight
beneath sweet smiles
and a melody
that only angels could sing

i see you.
my eyes can see through your skin
that's laced together with spite
double-knotted with narcissism
and a passion to be
the only thing
people see.

i don't see what most do
when i hear you, i hear the growl
from your throat that threatens to escape
with each lie you profess.
when i see you
i see the cement you smother over
the green tinge to your face
i see the smile that doesn't reach your eyes
i see the emptiness within
that you try to fill
with a caricature of someone pure
someone innocent -
someone else.

perhaps you're scared
that you're not interesting enough
for people to like you without lies
perhaps you're right.

i may wear my heart on my sleeve
but my tongue
is made of thorns
that'll pierce through your falsities
and expose your flesh
for all to see
leaving you naked
bare.
just remember,
lies can't cover up
someone who is no longer there.

THE SWIMMER

Melissa Lee Ramos

Jumping in, submerged, the water flows over my head. Bubbles escape as I sink. My hair swirls around me as soft as angel's wings, twirling around like leaves on a breezy day.

Moving my limbs, I move ever so slowly. The slightly chilled, clear liquid pushes and pulls, pulls me down with the weight of gravity, pushes as I swim.

The glorious calm engulfs all thoughts.

I am no longer. I exist as a fish, a mermaid with no destination. No thoughts. No worries. Just myself: a simple being gliding through the non-existent waves.

The sunlight bending and breaking as it hits the water sends ripples of color dancing down to the bottom of the pool.

Closing my eyes, I let go. I just want to feel. It's like being in a down-filled bed. Light and feathery. Soft and gentle. The liquid trickles into my ears, causing a sound not unlike that of the voice of a seashell. The gentle hum like the soft calls of seagulls at daybreak.

My body rises to the surface. My face breaks free. Gulping a lungful of air, I turn and push myself back to the bottom. With eyes closed tight, I imagine the fathomless depths of the ocean and wish that's where I was.

If I were a braver soul, I would do it—dive into the murky sea and let the currents keep me in their hold. A forever mermaid.

For now, I'm content in the shallow-ish pool. I can only get so lost, so far, before reality brings me back.

But right now, here in this moment, my soul is home. My mind stops churning. The tabs are all closed. The lights go out, and I exist in an existence-less place.

I'm a lone fairy floating, lost in the garden. A single star in a starless night.

The only being in the whole world.

I'm startled out of my respite by a sudden earthquake shaking movement.

My body bounces around like a buoy caught adrift in a stormy sea. Eyes flying open, huge and wide, momentarily unsure of where I am, I see the ripples of my once peaceful water. Another person has jumped into my lonesome world, my safe haven.

My calm has ended.

Eyes burning from the toxic chlorine, I make my way back to the surface. Taking a huge gulp of hot air, I sigh. The other person does not acknowledge my presence. It's as if I don't really exist.

I am one with the water.

Wading to the wall, I push off with all my might, hurtling myself through the water like a giant whale.

My thoughts return with a vengeance. I can't escape them for long. Pretending to be a mermaid, I am swimming for my life, racing against time and the current of the ocean that is my mind.

I push myself faster, harder, keep going, keep going.

My muscles burn, arms and legs tire, but I can't stop. I mustn't stop. The monsters in my head are chasing me. I can't outrun them for long.

I try to push away the countless worries and anxieties for as long as I can.

Eventually, the body gives into exhaustion. I sink into the cool shadows of the water, gripping the wall to avoid drowning, as my vision blurs.

I overdid it.

My thoughts stop. I wait for the beating of my heart to calm, to return to normal. The sunlight beams downs and warms my face.

I am calm once again.

My soul is rejuvenated by the sweet water. The gentle rocking from the miniature waves created by the other swimmer almost put me to sleep. It's a lovely lullaby I wish would go on forever.

As the sun begins to set in the sky, I watch as the other swimmer leaves my temporary home. I close my eyes, take a deep breath, and sink to the bottom.

I stay down as long as I can.

When my lungs are about to burst, I carry my limbs back to the surface. I dive again and again, sitting, waiting, not thinking.

When my skin is all wrinkled, my hair in tangles, the night creeping in, I climb out of the water. I walk away slowly as if I'm leaving something precious behind—a piece of my heart.

Until tomorrow when I can return to the open arms of the pool, I'll move through the ever-changing world, silently taking what comes at me, trying to appease the monsters in my head.

Until my next swim when I can return home.

BREAKDOWN

Lynne Shayko

My brain was a machine
That ate problems
And forced dissonance into logical equations.

But then it broke.
Then the System broke me.

I was a speedboat.
I metamorphosed into a raft
Without oars,
Floating naked in a stream.

I was a missile.
I became a parachute
Victim to a storm.

I was a force.
I became a dandelion.

I was Potential.
I became a lockbox of memories.
All my vulnerabilities,
All the inappropriate thoughts
Locked into compartments
Until I found the key
To open them.

The key was always within myself.
It had just been swallowed so deeply

That it took years of inner searching
To find it.

I think I have found the key.
Now it is only un-riddling the origami
Of my compartmented mind,
Un-puzzling the pieces of me,
Forcing phrases into paragraphs,
Creating my whole self again.

THE TWISTER

By Zoe Wall

On awakening, an endless fog engulfs me,
Full of my night's despair that slipped into my dreams.

I was lost within its turmoil, alone in darkness' grip,
I could not escape that place, however familiar it felt.

Get a grip, hold on, move on, you will be fine,
Those voices twisting turbulently, becoming faster with my breath.

My mirror does not lie when the sunken eyes stare,
Each flaw left uncovered for all of it to see.

It engulfed me last night, don't you see,
It's a friend and an enemy,
A twisted state that is now
My only fate.

Leaving me shattered.

Alone.

Every morning it twists.

BROKEN

By Sharmila Mitra

Money is missing.
The bag
The money-bag.
Hey!
My money.

Who's that
Standing like a fool?

Have you seen
My money-bag?
Was under, no, under,
Yes!
Under pillow.
Saw it.

Hey you!
Saw it myself.
Damn...

No! Don't want lunch!
Want my money!

"Dad, you had no money."

Hah! Fool!
Know how much
I got monthly?
Got any idea?

"Dad, listen..."

Shut-up.
Took away my phone too!
I need talk.
Hey, get Sam, now!

"Dad, Sam..."

Are you stupid?
Or mad?
Sam.
Sam, my friend.

"Dad, he's no more."

More fool you.
You want to
Keep me like this.

Took all my money.
My money is gone.
And

Who are you?

Hey, get me ice-cream, okay?
Don't mind, eh?

** The kind of dialogue I often had with my father for three years after he was diagnosed with dementia is the backdrop of this broken sort of poem.

OBSESSIVE-COMPULSIVE DEMONS.

By D.M. Woon

Oh, to be free of ritual. Take the chains and
break them, lead them to the rooftop and cast them
skyward, let them spiral from your hand.
Every single day, the seconds, as you've passed them,
still mock you with each tick and tock,
still hold you in the vice as Obsessive-Compulsive Demons hiss
in your ear, please check the lock.
Value security far greater when the devil's kiss
escapes his arid lips and burrows in your neck.

Check. A million times, check.
Oven off, gas off, water off, windows shut.
Mantra repeated so that you may silence the doubt-
please check the lock -the doubt that flutters in your gut
until the mantra is repeated, repeated, hiss, kiss, shout.
Locked, locked, locked, locked, locked, locked.
Six times over and to a familiar tune, so that
if your visual recollection is later blocked,
verify your actions in B-flat.
Everything is done, on song you rely.

Deny. The doubts of The Demons, deny.
In music, in rhythm; the ritual, the rhyme.
Seconds still mock, tick-tock, check the lock.
On shuffle, same playlist, same song, every time.
Rewind, fast forward, play, pause, stop.
Demons hiss, devil's kiss, never miss a beat.
Enemies in your head as long as you're on your feet.
Repeat. Tomorrow our song will play again.

ME? MENTAL ILLNESS? WELL I NEVER!
By Tina Cooper

The good thing about singlehandedly trying to save the world and ending up sat on the floor of a farmhouse kitchen in the middle of nowhere, being stared at by the family that live there, is that they call the police.

You get sectioned, and help comes your way. Lots and lots of lovely help.

I know this because it happened to a dear friend of mine, a friend who is now well but rather embarrassed by it all. She shouldn't be.

It was clear what needed to be done, and a farm, with its crops and animals, was obviously the best place to start the new-and-improved world. My friend need not be embarrassed. If the end of the world was nigh, I'll go wherever she goes because she has a plan—a good one at that.

Then there was the friend of a friend who was convinced he'd started the Gulf War—he hadn't, by the way. He too got help and was soon tickety boo.

Then there's me.

I'd not felt well for a while, but my regular trips to the doctor's proved fruitless. I was no nearer to knowing what the hell was going on. I was sent for tests, as one doctor thought I may have had a stroke. I hadn't, which was nice, but I was in pain. I was tired to the point of feeling parts of me switch off.

My eyes would give up; they would decide they had enough of seeing shit for one day, so they'd just not bother. Yet, when tested, my eyes were fine.

I'd have panic attacks whilst asleep and, rather inconveniently, while I was awake, too. Much oddness occurred for no apparent reason.

Eventually, I stopped going to the doctor; it was getting embarrassing. I'd asked one if I was dying, and he chuckled.

"Yes, but not of this."

This? What was this?

I had come to the conclusion that I wasn't going to drop dead any time soon, so I decided to walk it off. The walk took three years, but I got there.

Onwards, I plodded, and I began to feel better-ish. Well, I felt better enough. The betterness I felt would have to do, and it did do—for a while.

Fast forward a few years.

I thought I was menopausal, so I took myself off to the doctor. I was not menopausal yet. I had blood tests, which were all fine, so it was deduced that I had myalgic encephalomyelitis, or M.E.

I was promptly referred to an M.E. clinic housed in a disability centre. A disability centre? Well, that made me feel awesome—not even a little bit.

M.E. had been mentioned previously, but it depended on which doctor I saw. One told me it was nonsense, and for reasons unknown, I decided to believe her. That was booboo.

Two hours, I was at the clinic. I was prodded and poked at no point ever, but I was given exercises to do.

My daily life was examined and pontificated, and then I saw the psychologist and a rather kind, but also rather intimidating, doctor who was clearly someone very important. He wore a very fancy suit and scared the bejesus out of me.

I told him everything. I told him stuff I'd long forgotten. I didn't need to because—if any of you have had the pleasure of talking to a psychologist, you will know—it is modern day witchcraft.

They already knew me. The real me. The me that even I didn't know. Spooky.

So the doctor, the clinical psychologist, the occupational therapist, and the physiotherapist walked into a bar. . . Not really; they had a meeting. They decided I had a right old case of the M.E.s, and they would help me to feel less shit. Hoorah!

I was called back for a debriefing with the psychologist who was to decide the best course of action.

What was meant to be one session with her turned into four—not a good sign—but eventually she plumped for cognitive behavioural therapy with a dash of graded exercise therapy thrown in. This starts next week.

I'm far more excited about this than I probably should be. I'm desperate to feel human again; I will take whatever they throw at me.

If I'm told to dress as a chicken and swim in the ocean, I will.

Any who, what I have come to realise is that my problems are of the mental variety. M.E. is the combination of many things: life experiences, illnesses, learnt coping behaviours that probably don't work anymore—if they ever did—and me just being me.

The symptoms of M.E. are different for each individual.

One lady I knew became bedridden and needed carers, thankfully, only for a short while. Another lost the use of her legs but had no pain at all. I had pain amongst other peculiar things.

'Tis all very confusing, but I'm beginning to understand the link between my mental and physical health. It would be fascinating if it were happening to someone else.

A few moons ago, I went through a period of shit, as we all do from time to time, but how I dealt with things was to not.

My walking it off hadn't walked it off after all. In fact, my way of coping was delaying my recovery. I was unknowingly milking it. I was keeping the ball of shite rolling. Who knew? When the going got tough, my fight-or-flight kicked in, but I'd never switched it off again because I didn't know how to. I'm going to have to learn how to turn it off, but I will need help.

When we were cavemen/women, our fight-or-flight response would kick in if we spotted a sabre toothed tiger. When the tiger went away, our fight-or-flight response would switch off.

Mine doesn't. I am ever ready for that sodding tiger, fired up just in case, and this is making me poorly.

Now, the point to all this waffling is that not everybody with a mental illness starts a war or prepares for the end of time. Not all have such obvious problems, and herein lies the problem.

Nobody believes you. Sometimes you don't believe you. People make assumptions and stop listening. You make assumptions, so you try to stop thinking. People stop listening, so you stop talking.

You don't listen to you, so why should anyone else? Then when you stop talking, you stop mending.

I know there is no quick fix for what goes on in my head, and I'm reliably informed that I may feel this way, to some extent, for the rest of my days, but I cannot express how it felt to be heard—to be believed.

My God, the relief!

Not only did the lovely white witch listen, but she told me I am worthy of a little assistance. For some reason, I thought I wasn't. She also told me that I don't have to do this alone; this, after I told her she wouldn't make me cry that day. I bawled like a baby with a dropped rattle.

That's the crutch of the matter; we need to talk about this stuff. If we don't, we think it's just us, that nobody else feels this way.

The reality is we all have tough times, and we all could do with a little help occasionally.

I thought, because I wasn't bat shit crazy like my marvellous, world-saving friend, I could just muddle on. That I didn't qualify or something; I thought I wasn't poorly enough.

Thankfully, my doctor didn't agree.

"If you have a tummy ache, you go to the doctor; you don't suffer unnecessarily. The same goes for mental health."

Go. Go now. See your doctor and tell them loudly and proudly that you are brave enough to ask for a helping hand.

INSOMNIA

By Helen Smith

what is it that brings
another restless dawn
the sun
horizon
soft light licks
around the curtain, warm
pulls my heavy eyes
away, away
from heavy nights
and sleep is a friend I
have not seen
holding
the dark

my love you are sleeping
so soundly
wrapped in this long morning
softly
the moon
a kiss, among constellations
fades as we move
to the day
burning
away the mist

I am not rested, night
do not leave me
cocoon me
embrace me

you watched me cold, and now
you turn away
away
my body aches
my mind
so far from resting

soft, the earth is soft
your hands
a silent gift
I go, I go
another day
longing
for the sweet, deep stillness
of sleep

SECONDHAND

Isabella Mansfield

nobody gets excited over
socks for Christmas
they're a need
never a want
just something you have
a side salad
ordered out of
obligation because
"you know you should"
but don't really want it

Maybe it says something
about me that I buy
all of my own clothes
second hand
not because it's a better deal
but gently used
in perfectly good
condition
(maybe a little faded
worn at the seams)

then suddenly unwanted;
this is what I identify
within my life, feeling
discarded, a poor fit
sold for a buck fifty
not really needed
but a bargain

and maybe there's
a little more life there
but it is not worth much

SOS

Outspoken St. Monk

I maintain my own hell
pay rent on it
even have my own guard dog, too
it's a dingy place
buts it's comfortable, I'm use to it
been here for as long as I can remember
it's home to me, all I've really known

I'd rather suffer for nothing, apparently
than suffer for a worthy cause
but that's not true, I'm bullshittin' you
I'm just stuck in a groove
I've given up on catching a ride
but this walk, buddy, is cold
unbearable at times
it's like a loop, I keep seeing
the same damn things

I try and change them
and for a bit I have myself fooled
but something stirs beneath
The Loch Ness Monster or something

BAM! BAM! BAM!

I'm back at square one
face in my palm crying
drawing circles on the wall

It's my hell, though, and I'll fight
to the death for it
because I'm lost
too stubborn to ask for help
I'm an unbreakable man
no one needs to understand me
not even myself
back away

Save your tears

For someone who cares

"SUFFERING IN SECRET"
Chanson Antonio Byrd

I'm scared to move on
Not because I'm afraid to love again
But because I'm unwilling to let myself get hurt again
I'm guarded because I was once unguarded
I let too many people in
Desperation was my bread and butter
Loneliness was my food and drink
Depression became an appendage
Hanging onto me like a lovesick teenager who found his crush
Now I built a wall as thick as Fort McHenry
Layered to withstand the darts that may come against me
So I sit back secretly admiring the beautiful creations
Of the female persuasion
But like a locked diary, I won't reveal my inner secrets
Fondness has become a fairy tale
Affection feels like an abstract idea from Aesop's fables
Liking someone feels like a large mistake
Love feels like lust on steroids
Lord, heal my wounded heart
That I may know how to experience this thing called love
Without hindering the process for she who truly adores me
And lead me in the way that I must go
That I may serve you in a more excellent way

RIBBONLESS

Paul Chambers

blurred ribbons
streaking around me
f a s t motion
others
succeeding
continually
their life colours
a twinkling rainbow
burnished things
and perfect lives
creating joyful fences
joy filled offenses
penning me in
and I stand
still
and still
I, stilted and
f a l l e n
I focus
on all that I shouldn't
and none
that I should
ears deaf
to proffered help
eyes blind
to gifts bestowed
back turned
black
to a bright future

all I see
in this glossy walled
prison of my
failings
is the potential
to fail, and flail
flop or die
or
flop
and die
rainbows ringing
singing at
this thing
m y
   l o w
      e b b
and reflect
as I cannot
with light
refracted
my life
redacted

PRESCRIPTION

Clare Heather Currie

Eyes come, go:
screen, hands, screen, face, screen, me?

You ask for the potted history:
fifty-second film-wrapped setback on a plate.

It is outside, separate. It is not yours.
no, it's not yours.

You would have to mangle a whole body
into a head, into a shoulder, into a lung –

Stretching down with pinky toe,
ring toe, until every toe
and membrane mimicked mine.

Until your calves – caught,
knees – translated onto knees
(torn cruciate ligament on the right.)

Until your flanks deciphered soft grazes
on the lodes,
on the hair-wisps of thighs.

Midriff overlapping midriff, fingering
every episode, exposure on the soft,
Linea belly Negra line.
This line is my line.
This face is my line.

You can't transpose a middle –
every cell: event imprint
a rib, deltoid – equally weighted – eagerness / dis ease.

A chest – areola-circled and sucked clean of milk,
like the milk: infusing growth / feeling
into bellies, bones.

You can't map a muscle memory of arms, hands -
warred in sport and
loss-circled in grief.

Or an ecstasy that rockets in the throat, announces to the head
to be moved by art, a one-off action,
or by uncomplicated, childlike joy.

And you can't become a body –
lying on a dark bed. When everything is out of reach
and can't quite be grappled with either.

And you can't become a body –
lying on a bed. Become a body, when everything is out of reach
lying on a bed. Become a body, when everything is out of reach.
Become a body that can't
quite be grappled with either.

You can't, you can't, you can't.

So you prescribe these pills instead.

"THOUGHTS"

Moriah

If only I could sleep without the constant flood of thoughts;
They fill my head
I turn in bed
My mind twists into knots.

I cannot drive to emptiness, the cavern of my soul;
The words collide
I cannot hide
Their darkness fills me whole.

I don't know what to do right now, to finally get some rest;
My hands are cold
The night is old
There's aching in my chest.

I don't know what will happen when the new day comes at last;
I turn my head
And wait in dread
For noise and night to pass.

BLUE COLLAR CRAZY
JD Hyde

To speak of being a man, you must talk about employment. To work is to be a man.

Well, it is in the societies who will read this.

Our lives are wrapped around our careers. Often, men spend more time at work than we do at home. We start as early in our lives as we can, and we keep going until retirement, sometimes death.

Many of us would prefer the latter than to be useless.

It is not that we enjoy toiling our lives away to make other people money or that we are avoiding the family that we rarely see. It is because in Western society, to be a man is to work. It often doesn't matter what job; the trash collector is held with the same regard as the IT tech. We nod at each other with an understanding that we are equals

.

As a man with a mental illness, though, you are not an equal.

Often, people, good people, who try to be fair, believe that to have a mental illness is to be untrustworthy.

How can you trust a man whose brain cannot be relied on? It's terrifying, for a crazy man can kill us all. He can snap at any moment.

The good people bring this to the job where the mentally ill are trying to work. I do know that these thoughts are not purposeful. The good people cannot control their thoughts anymore than I can, but I've also learned a few things over the twenty-five years I've been in the workforce.

I have learned that I have a name that is not on my birth certificate: "Crazy James."

I have heard this name at every job I've ever had. Never when they know that I am within earshot, of course.

There's a whole fun list that I can now answer to: Psycho, Nutjob, Wing Nut.

The list goes on and on. Imaginative isn't it?

Then, there are the looks on their faces when you ask them to find something new. They are five-year olds caught in the cookie jar.

To complain to management is of no use. An insane man's word against a sane man's? You may as well scream your complaint into a cave. At least then you'll get an echo.

I have also learned to work by myself. No one wants to work with a psycho even if he is good at his job. It's also safe to say you better be good if you plan on working while mentally ill. For that matter, you better be better than anyone else on the job site.

To keep your job, you will study it and learn any trick you can to be the fastest and most skilled.

I have never left a position that didn't have to hire at least two people to replace me.

However, don't think that you're going places with all this hard work.

A promotion is not going to happen, and nothing is more fun than hearing that you didn't get it. Well, other than being told you'll train the person who did.

In each job, you will think, This time will be different. This time, people will treat you as they say they want to be treated. It will be fair; you will do well.

Then you will slip. They will find out that you are not one of the good people, and those you have become friends with will turn on you.

You will be a pariah until you move on down the road to play the entire game over again.

When I started writing this, I wanted to end on a positive note, telling everyone that we can change this. We can't. They will crush our souls worse than the illness does, and they will laugh while they do it.

We are probably beaten.

I doubt if we can change even one person, much less the world, but that doesn't mean that we shouldn't try.

We must stand.

Every time we hear an insult, we must say, "No. I am a person who deserves to be treated with respect."

Every time.

We probably won't win the war, but we can leave one less battle for someone else to fight.

"DIAGNONSENSE"

Lynne Shayko

I fit every label
but none.
I wish they would realize
I lie between
the lines of the DSM-V.

Would you walk over me
with sharp, stiletto words
or measure my pulse,
fingers at my wrist?

Would you be my savior?
Then choose your method:
purify me with water
or antiseptic.

You may
plaster nametag labels on my chest
or call me "Lynne."

I must warn you;
the stickers fall off
eventually,
but this paper proclaims

I own this name.

TRANSFORMATION
(A PANTOUM)

By Miriam Ruff

I need to take just one small step to start,
A gesture toward the greater goal of life;
I'm scared about how I will come apart,
But waiting seems to be so charged with strife.

A gesture toward the greater goal of life,
In times to come I'll fill my destiny;
But waiting seems to be so charged with strife,
The knife whose twists and turns will gut what's me.

In times to come I'll fill my destiny,
To step beyond myself I must then try;
The knife whose twists and turns will gut what's me,
I'll vanish in the blinking of an eye.

To step beyond myself I must then try,
To take the reins and guide myself now through;
I'll vanish in the blinking of an eye,
But I'll emerge again once whole and new.

To take the reins and guide myself now through,
I'm scared about how I will come apart;
But I'll emerge again once whole and new,
I need to take just one small step to start.

(c) 2017 Miriam Ruff

PROGRESS

By Sandy Wardrop

It's intolerable
Getting from A to B
It's insufferable
When you're just four and three

Trudge, trudge, trudge...
Through the fudge of the myriad muds

With the ten-year olds towering over
Looking down on the boy who's just seven
On you trudge, trudge, trudge...
And the soil sublimes into sludge

Then you're cresting
At the top of a hill
It's like resting
Only not standing still
Children jesting
Then they start testing
Who'll tumble like Jack or like Jill?

Still a trudge.
Trudge.
"What a glorious true pilgrimage!

"To be out in the air
"Who among us would dare
"To question this wonderful trudge?"

Me.
And my soul
And my legs which are taking the toll

And as you think it gets better
The ground it gets wetter
But it's fine all the while you don't
F
  a

  a

   a faaAAAAAAAAAAAAAAAAAAAAAaaaaa
    a

    a

    a

    a
l
Then feel the smack
Of the whack of the backpack
In the small of your back
Having tracked at the back of the pack
For so long

Now you've stumbled
And it's you who is taking the tumble - oh

It's intolerable
Feeling small and so judged
It's insufferable
When you've trudged, and you've trudged, and you've trudged.

Brush it off
Keep on going
Brush it off

Though you're knowing
All the tall ones are sniggering and laughing
Giggling at the silhouette boy made of mud

But you trudge.
You have to trudge.
For 21 years feeling judged

And it's insufferable
Getting from A to B
It's intolerable
Feeling four and just three

For so long.
But you're wrong.
Soon it's not quite so difficult to see

We're all trudging and trudging and trudging
On
Through the minefield of everyone judging

But once you learn to look up
With no ten-year olds sniggering
And you see the sky
And think what a glorious day - what a glorious life
To be out in the air
Who among us would dare
To question this true pilgrimage?

And the trudge becomes slower and easier
And your feet become simpler to budge

It's not so insufferable

Getting from A to B
Less intolerable
When you're free to just be.

A TALK WITH DEPRESSION

By Aidan Van Den Bergh

Wake up and get out,
But it's cold out there.
Look around at all that's about,
But it's too dark, I fear.
Face the day!
But there's nowhere to hide.
Fine, then stay!
But it's too frightful inside.
Then stand up and fight.
But there's no one to aid.
A coward's response: flight.
But if not, they'll soon invade.
There're no such things as demons.
But then who's holding this gun?
It's an easy path to freedom.
But my nerves are undone.
You're on your own, and you know it,
But all I ask for is light.
You'll learn to outgrow it.
But my days are all night.
Now, now. There, there.
But I know this won't end.
Well, if it's too much to bear.
Goodbye, my old friend.

THREE STRIPES FROM THE SEAM AND STRAIGHT ON TILL MORNING

By Carol Alena Aronoff

The right way to make a bed.
For some devotees, precision
is religion, the lure of perfection
a martyr's addiction. Free-flowing,
forays into the formless, anathema
to the architecture of such an ordered
mind. A world of right angles, smooth
edges, military corners. No geographical
irregularities. Smart delineations between
too much and too little. No room for whimsy,
for mismatched socks, stray dust motes,
threads hanging down from a French seam
or hem. A gold-leaf frame slightly off kilter,
an asymmetric smile. Is enough to set off
urgent alarms.

THE FOG

By Mrs. Pratima Apte

Borrowing Sherin Mary Zachariah's coinage, "The Mist of Myself"

Alzheimer's runs in my family
I dread the future
How do I escape it?

I eat a balanced diet
Follow fixed rest-work-sleep patterns
But this gnawing fear never goes
Should I get myself genetically tested to find out for sure if I carry it?

Marry?
I cannot
Let me limit the damage by being single

Does it strike in old age only?
I must write down every detail of my life up till now, lest I forget
Start and maintain a diary for all the remaining days in my life
Make a photo album of my babyhood, childhood, adulthood

This diaphanous veil will slowly descend on my psyche
I will clutch at straws to brush it aside
The mist will overpower me someday

No! I cannot have that happening to me
Don't laugh
It is not an impossible happening
It could strike you, too

Just imagine being lost in a fog,
You are trying to catch your shadow, just a step out of grasp
Swirling, whirling around you

You cannot see your feet, either
Nor where you are going, standing
The ground beneath you uneven
The road leading nowhere
Is there a gorge, precipice, or a sheer wall ahead?

Am I alone on this lonely planet?

Where's my family, loved ones, friends?
Have they deserted me?
Or have I them?
Will you recognise me from the identity parade?
Will I be reduced to a number?

Like the newborn baby

Search hard for me
Look out for me
Return me to myself on this side of the mirror

A DAY IN THE LIFE OF A DEPRESSIVE
By Lindsey Woodward

My eyes feel cemented shut, my eyelids weighed down by concrete blocks.

This bed is my refuge. These blankets are my shield from the outside world, from life. Yet they do very little to warm me from the painful chills of existence.

The hurt is inescapable in waking hours. Sleep is my only true solace, a temporary reprieve in which I immerse myself with the silent desperation of one who has lost their will to live.

I can't recall the last time I smiled genuinely or didn't force a laugh. The flesh on my cheeks has become dry and flaky from the tears that pour out in salty torrents. This is not melodrama. This is my reality; the ineffable misery that has loathsomely become routine.

Words are futile communicators of this deep, endless ache.

I know I should get out of bed, at least for a bit, but I can't. I can't seem to find a point, not an iota of motivation. Everything that once brought me joy, even contentment, has been robbed from me by an unseen thief residing in my mind's dankest corner.

Merely lifting off the covers has become an Olympian feat. Responding to text messages exhausts me. Personal hygiene has been shelved and forgotten.

People say, "Exercise more! Eat healthy!" How am I supposed to work out when getting myself to the toilet is a gruelling task? When pouring a glass of water to swallow my pills feels like running a marathon on the hottest day in August? How am I supposed to eat healthy when all food tastes like ash, and I can barely get out of bed, let alone go to the crowded grocery store where strangers too can see how worthless I've become?

Sometimes, I'll put on a funny TV show, hoping to distract myself from my sadness, but I always end up feeling worse because I don't laugh when I know I normally would.

My once technicolour world has faded out to, not even black and white, but monochrome shades of grey that bleed into a dull haze. It feels like this depression will never relent. The light that once shone from the tunnel's end has receded to a pinprick before being totally extinguished.

Despite my depressive states growing progressively more severe as I age, they do always pass, eventually. Usually, with the right medication tweak but sometimes just from the passage of time or a change of seasons.

I am blessed to have such a strong network of support surrounding me during these times. I need constant reminders that things will improve because I come to a point where I no longer believe it is possible.

Yet, regardless of how permanent these periods seem, they, like everything else in life, are subject to change, and eventually the dark tunnel's end shows signs of a faint flicker which slowly, but steadily, expands until I can't discern the tunnel from the sunlight shining all around me.

'OVERDOSE'

James Donnelly

My poisoned pens
are all poised at me
Because I fail to be present
for others regularly

I let the nastiest parts of me
the critic, the boss, the bully
get in the way of me
fully

I can't connect
in the ways I wish I would

Cos that 'I'
is always in the way
The 'I' filled
with self-doubt, dismay

Who block
the view
of a
needful you

And I became
another mouthpiece
who couldn't
offer peace

Because this brain
is masturbatory
Same old
self-fucking story

There is a game I play
Try to make myself okay

But it all ends
in a big comedown
Mania will always
end with a frown

As the dip and the drop
kicks in again
and I run low
on serotonin

Hold out for the peaks
I declare
But instead
I stop and stare

As I drown in inches
of dirty water
Not prop myself up
Like I ought to

Cos the Villain
is an easy role
when you don't believe
you have a soul.

HABITS

Christopher Stolle

I see you've started smoking again.
You've developed an odd predilection
for walking with a cane. You've also
rediscovered driving, but I never see you
thumbing through fresh fruit or books.
I rarely find you lingering in places
where we've not spent any time together.

Do you go anywhere for anyone but me?

Maybe these are spots you enjoyed
when you were young. How much
has changed? Can you still find your way?
What memories greeted you? What friends
awaited your arrival? Who will come later?
Did someone else have your heart then?

Do you know if anyone else looks for you?

Why didn't I ask these questions when
you were here? Would you have answered?
I wonder why you rarely had words for me.
But I'll keep looking for you. I'll search
through crowds, across restaurants, and even
in spots where I feel your eyes watching me.

I won't stop until you recognize me.

THE DOG

Rob Harding

She says it'd been there for weeks
Sniffing round the garbage
Scratching in the dirt
Its dark, shaggy hackles superimposed
Against the sickly ring of the moon
I didn't notice it
She says it barked in the night
Or howled
Its scarred head tossed back
A guttural reverberation rattling out of its ragged throat
But I hadn't heard it
She says it watched her
Followed her
When she went out
When she came back from the shops
When she played with the kids in the garden
It was always just out of her eye-line
She says
But she knew it was there
Lurking in the foliage
Hunched in the brambles
Growling in the hedgerows
I'd not seen it
Not until the other week

It entered our home
Sidled up to her
Like it knew her
Belonged to her

Or her to it
Still I didn't see it as such
I saw its prints, though
Saw the markings of its claws on the walls
Smelt its damp, heady musk in the air
Dark clumps of coarse hair
Caught in my throat
She didn't mention it at first
The vast, dark padding thing
So I didn't mention it either
Maybe it was all in my head
But it wasn't
Not in mine
It wasn't my black dog

Eventually, one night,
As she lay in bed
This rough brute sprawled across her chest
Squeezing moist air
From bellow bag lungs
She wept and told me of the dog
Then things made sense

It didn't take long for me to become accustomed to it
It curled in the corner of our room
And I regarded it no more
Than I regarded the wardrobe
Or her slippers
Or our baby's crib

She tells me I'll never understand it
I'll never know what it wants
It's not me it picks at when it hungers

It's not even slightly my black dog

I resented not just the dog
I grew impatient and angry with her
Why could she not just forget it
Like I could?
After all, it was her it'd followed into the house
It wasn't my black dog!

Last month it blocked her
In the downstairs loo
Where we keep the medicine

I knew I couldn't defeat it alone
But I didn't need to let it in
I didn't need to pass it scraps from the table
Provoke it into baring its snaggled, yellow fangs
I didn't need to just let it sleeping lie
I could have insisted we call a professional
To help remove it
But I didn't
And it kept eating
And it got bigger
While I satisfied my soul
With the knowledge
The mantra
That it wasn't my black dog

Then we moved

We left that house and left the dog
She gladly fled from it
And I certainly had no interest

In leaving breadcrumbs
It wasn't, after all, my black dog
It had nobody now
It'd die of starvation and neglect
It was nobody's black dog anymore

Last Tuesday, I found dark hairs on the rug

CRACKPOT

Carol Tierney

Crackpots - That's what they used to call us
Our crack pot ideas not the happy thoughts you can safely voice
I wonder if they know how right they were
I know I am cracked, broken
It doesn't matter how much time I spend filling myself with happy thoughts
They all leak away through the cracks
Soon I will be empty again

Filling the cracks is a never-ending chore
Sometimes the filler is soft and crumbles away
Sometimes it sets hard like Chinese gold
But one little knock is all it ever takes
Drop me and I shatter
However many times I am put back together, I am always cracked

A MESSAGE TO MY MIND
Chellsey

You betrayed me. You broke me.
You stole the pieces of who I was.

You took me.
You twisted me.
You made me into half the person I prided myself on being.

At the age of thirteen, I was left to cope alone with the scared truths cutting left, blaming myself for something that was, but wasn't really, in my control.

Being labelled in Junior High as that freak with the emo scars.

Until the day my seventeen-year-old self split my wrist open.

That was the moment I exposed what was inside of me, and the moment I saw what was beneath my flesh. There it was on my body, in plain view; yet still, no one understood.

It was like suicide wasn't real.

My blood, an inconvenience to my parent; my ripped flesh, a hindrance to my current boyfriend.

Something that would later be used against me to excuse his cheating.

Because what sane person would ever do such a thing?

That night left me with a deep fear and disgust, not just with what my eyes experienced, but with what it exposed inside of me. Instead of cutting to ease my pain, I purged it from my body.

My arms had been destroyed, and over time, you made the choice to kill what was within.

Chest heaving, stomach burning, eyes watering; the compliments on my weight loss reinforced my new compulsion.

Was I really sick? Or was I doing it to myself?

It would take me four years to realize that those weren't two questions, but two parts of one.

Day after day, you took more of me—my pure flesh, my healthy teeth and body—until my mind became a total loss.

You gave me nineteen years of close to normal, allowing me to finally adapt into myself and bad choices, before stealing my world away and forcing me to rebuild on a faulty foundation and with rotting walls.

Any progress was unreliable; the work was for nothing.

The walls deteriorated further; the foundation crumbled beyond repair, but from the outside, things appeared normal.

I'm not really a house, though, so when that part of me died, no one understood.

Cancer wasn't killing me; I didn't lose a leg. I didn't contract a disease; I looked fine, so I must be fine.

Explain that to a guy you're dating while your body is kidnapped by some foreign intruder.

They broke in, beat me to the ground, and stole my ability to breathe. I was left lying on the floor, suffocating in my own attack, not sure why my lungs were burning. Why my chest was tight and my asthma was activated, unprovoked, to leave me throwing up only saliva blocking my throat.

All while I was examined by a man who now saw the freak show I attempted to contain.

Without warning, you started World War Three against me.

My body had taken damage already, and my borders were unsecured, vulnerable. My walls needed to be thicker, higher, tougher. They needed to protect me from you; by default, from any person who could possibly see anything but misery in me.

You had the key, though, the secret code. You lived within these stronger walls, attacking and retreating, unexpected and unprovoked.

What happened? They would ask, but I didn't have an answer.

But you knew that because you isolated me and gave me something that should leave a physical warning.

If I had contracted a disease, I would have a treatment to follow. If I had cancer, the doctors would have a million steps in place. If I lost a leg, there would be an explanation as to what was going on.

Instead, life gave me an incurable disease of the mind; one of those terminal ones which slowly deteriorate until only a shell is left. Until a shell is buried, leaving only memories behind.

Because I didn't get cancer. I didn't lose a leg. I didn't catch something.

So I should just stop.
So I should just be positive.
So I should just get over it.
So I shouldn't be complaining; others do have real conditions.

Because I don't exist.

Mental illness is a part of who I am, a part that isn't going to go away with an antibiotic or magic pill. It's never going to simply disappear; there is no cure. It's a terminal disease of the mind.

When they say my issues aren't real, they're saying a part of me isn't real; part of me is a myth.

If I had one of those other diseases, all I would need to do is make a phone call and be taken care of.

Family and friends would group to support me through my time of struggle, and help me through it.

I could stumble into a doctor who would bend heaven and hell to get me the help I need.

I'd be going through a trauma but wouldn't be alone.

Not with bipolar.

When you have anxiety, you're passed over. Look at a flickering candle, work out, stop having insomnia, and just sleep.

When you have panic attacks, you're disregarded. Stop being tense, take a hot shower, take a bath, don't think about it.

When you cry to yourself at night, begging your body for sleep, you're talked down to. Turn off the TV, read a book, stop thinking so much.

When you're depressed, you're inconsiderate. Take a vitamin, have a drink, work out.

Not when you're suicidal.

When you're suicidal, you must be seeking attention.

When they tell me my condition isn't real, they take another part of my life.

Stop overreacting. Never mind that I physically cannot make myself breathe normally.

Stop being a downer. Never mind that I cannot just be happy on another's command.

All a downward spiral.

Stop being yourself; stop being who you are.
Stop trying to accept yourself for who you are, and just be someone else.
Someone normal.
Someone better.

Because I don't really exist; you made sure of that.

DEPRESSION

By Bipul Banerjee

Stealthily
In dark corners of the heart
Is settling a germ-plasm of despair
Nurtured in silence
Suffering by guilt
Ridiculed beyond measures
Joys of life in fading spectrum
Shades of grey covering glee
Every passing day
Pushes life towards circles dark
All emotions in negative shades
Urge to cocoon
Thrust to end
The victim walks on
A diminishing thread
The tight lips
The lone shudders
Doors of loneliness
Bolted strong
A friend
A guide
A mentor
Has to knock
Break the ice
Let's talk
Let's shoulder the burdened soul
Push the button
Erupt the volcano
Allow the lava to flow

Burn the negativity to ashes
Bring back life
On autumnal branches
Help them again to grow

BIPOLAR

By Peter Hickman

I am one flawed individual;
A real-life Jekyll and Hyde.
On the one hand, I'm worthless.
On the other, I'm denied.
Denied a brain that functions
In accordance with the norm
And left to battle this life
In a chemically-induced storm.

Depression makes me vulnerable
And at times, I lose the plot;
Fearing I can't continue
Without a substance to block.
Block the path of the reaper
Whose grim presence I can feel
Even when I am manic
And am on the cusp of my ordeal.

FINGERNAILS

By Helen Smith

Silver moons
Crescents at the end of a soft pink sky

Tap against piano keys
Keeping time, lost in the melody

Blunt knives
Gouging scarlet furrows across ivory wrists

Crescents, grubby eclipses
Searching, reaching, holding, touching

Bitten, harsh
These ends of me

I am alone

NIGHT NOW FALLING
(AN ENGLYN PENFYR)

By Miriam Ruff

A whisper in my mind - it draws me in
Life's naught but sin, never kind
with thoughts on endless rewind

In madness trapped - not able to escape
Upon the nape, noose now wrapped
pulled so tight it leaves me sapped

Drumbeats rolling - the end is within sight
In dark night, death extolling
the bells for me now tolling

The legacy I leave - such thoughts I keep
For them I weep, even grieve
there will be no last reprieve

(c) 2017 Miriam Ruff

A DAY IN THE LIFE OF BIPOLAR MANIA

By Lindsey Woodward

My eyes burst open as my entire body is flooded with electric energy. I check the time. 4 a.m., despite having gone to bed a mere two hours prior, but two hours is an accomplishment when many nights whiz passed utterly sleepless.

I don't need to rest when I feel this way. Sleeping is a waste of time when there is so much to accomplish, experience, and, unwittingly destroy.

I leap out of bed and immediately light a cigarette before boiling the kettle for coffee. Even though I'm strung higher than a kite in a tornado, the more stimulants I can consume, legal or otherwise, feel necessary—anything to intensify my buzz.

I know what I'll do today. I'll write a novel.

Or make every single craft I've ever saved on Pinterest.

Or talk to every person who will listen to my genius rambling insights for hours while I chain smoke.

Or I'll take my coloured chalk and decorate every town sidewalk with my masterpieces. If it rains tonight, great! Blank canvases for tomorrow!

Or I could try to score some drugs from that guy I swore I'd never associate with again. Drink with him and probably have sex with him, even though I have a long-term partner whom I love and cherish deeply.

I scrap the creative projects and embark on a frenzied walk, adorned in my most outrageous outfit, my makeup resembling that of a clown on LSD.

The tree leaves sparkle and speak to me. I see God in everything: every wind rustled grass blade, every child's nervous smile, every cloud wisp lining the sky above me. I am a messenger and I must spread the good word to the entire world.

I post grandiose claims and revelations on social media, desperate to reach as many people as possible. Friends and family members reach out to me with deep concern. I respond assuredly with:

"No, I'm fine! I'm great! Never felt better! You have nothing to worry about!"

"No. I'm not taking my meds. I need to be authentic. K, gotta go! Let's hang out soon, k? K, bye!"

I refuse to listen to reason. Nobody sees the world how I do. But they will. The apocalypse is coming, and they will thank me for preparing them.

I'm a vehicle of God. I'm a vehicle of God; they'll see and believe.

In the aftermath of a manic episode, cleaning up the wreckage and accepting and taking accountability for my actions is immeasurably difficult.

There are, inevitably, many people I love dearly whom I've hurt, many words uttered I wish I could take back, many consequences that I was unable to foresee. Sometimes relationships are destroyed, money has been blown on superfluous items, and the depressive crash is abysmal.

In retrospect, it's like watching a movie of myself, an actress who looks like me but acts in ways the healthy, more balanced me would never conceive.

CHARITÉ

By Bruce Millar

I move down
the bright corridor
clutching my small bouquet
as a woman shuffles
slowly past
eyes straight ahead
seeing somewhere else
somewhere far away
a thousand-yard stare
they called it
in Vietnam

Maybe it's the drugs
the lights are too bright
and hospital disinfectant
cannot begin to cover up
the hundreds of years
of pain in this place
my small bouquet
looks even smaller
in the empty hospital room
and so does my hurt friend
even smaller
It has come to this
she says
she is broken
by an aching sadness
that all of us know
but some of us hide

better than others
in places where the lights
are not so damn bright
like dim bars
and glowing cigarettes
and blue nightmares on TV
you think you will turn off
but never do

So we walk by the river
in the falling dark
and misting rain
and talk of minds
turning in circles
break free
I try to say
and look for a cafe
that's still open
turning in circles
until eventually we only
come back
to the hospital

The rain has stopped
under the yellow streetlight
I hear a woman's voice
very distantly
crying in pain
or sorrow or horror
on and on
turning in circles
I pretend she's not there
and tell a joke

--

(c) Bruce Millar 2.10.2013 Berlin, Germany

DARK AND DREARY

By: Nancy Xiong

Dark and dreary
Her demons crawl nearer
She's all alone
There's nobody there
She tries to find
A reason to stay alive
To start breathing
To start breathing
And as she weeps
We all wonder why
She's always crying
It's like she's dying
She's on her knees
And I'm running away
Don't want to see this
I don't want to see this

Chorus:
'Cause it affects me
When she's crying
I want to help her
But she won't listen
And now she's bleeding
And my heart is breaking
I don't want to see this
I don't want to be this

And through her eyes
Everything's black and white

Nothing fades
To her color-blind eyes
Ain't what she wants
And she don't understand
She's pushing borderline
I idolized
The woman she once was
So strong
In her faith and love
And now she's gone
Only her tears remain
To haunt me
Yes, to haunt me

Chorus
'Cause it affects me
When she's crying
I want to help her
But she won't listen
And now she's bleeding
And my heart is breaking
I don't want to see this
I don't want to be this

Chorus
'Cause it affects me
When she's crying
I want to help her
But she won't listen
And now she's bleeding
And my heart is breaking
I don't want to see this
I don't want to be this way

I WILL NOT SAY THE NAMES
(LIFE WITH DISSOCIATIVE IDENTITY DISORDER)

By Lynne Shayko

Who am I?
Who are we?
When I diminish, they grow stronger.
When I am too quiet, they shout.
When you speak to my deepest part,
You may meet someone else.

When the world almost breaks me,
My selves splinter and scatter.
I vanish into a cloud.
I appear on your doorstep.

I meet you as I walk the tightrope
Of a paper thin computer screen.
I collapse within the spaces
Between a paragraphed life.
I assemble myself
Into a poem.

I will not say the names
Of my other selves.
When I name them,
They scream.

UNTITLED

By Moriah

The night is hard, the night is long
When day is over, night is come
The fateful night, the hardest test
The dreams we chase are laid to rest.

Dark weighs heavy, hearts are cold
We wait for sunlight to unfold
To shine on us in glorious day
To tell us that it's all okay.

The night is long, the night is long
The hours slow, the pains drags on
But daybreak comes, the faithful friend
Our brokenness comes to an end.

DARK VOICES

Squeakypeewee01

The voices in the dark
Shout out eternal promises
Come to us
Come to us
The constant drum and repetition
Envious of those freedoms
No longer available
Years of listening to the forces
Of righteousness
Will the torment end
Or should the shackles be loosened?

This pit is not despair
A place of safety
It brings to light
All that is wrong with
The system
Irritating skin
From the burn of others' words
Time suspended
When speed is all that's asked.

Marks of time
Etched not on the walls
But in the lines of faces
Grey pallor
Yellow eyes
The lack of sunlight fades the mind
Passing bodies

From one room to the next.

People striving to co-exist
Yet hiding behind masks
The brick wall
Or the joker
Never revealing what's underneath
For terror lies there
Bowing low, on bended knee
To those who have the power
And strength to unlock the door.

The look of disdain
Given freely to the scum
But deep inside
They are ashamed of their own crimes.

It takes a moment
A lack in concentration
And you'll find yourself
Where only your nightmares have taken you.

Politics
No vote.

A way out is only a thought
That passes each and every
Day.

Getting by on minimalistic means
Tricks learned to show
Resilience and oppression
Tow the line,

Gain that trust
But darkness and voices yet
Resist the need to try much harder.

Noise, noise
It's far too much
Is there a place for this release?

The grating frustration
Nerves on edge
Closing eyes to fade out the anger
Looking at faces, teeth missing
Looking like broken
Sugar puffs.

Hygiene becomes a thing of the past
But for others, it's all they have.

Enveloping lives
Entwining desires
'Let them out'
'Set them free'
Offensive, though our looks are,
See inside and
The love they share
Will become evident.

Until you've seen inside these minds
Enjoy the dark
The voices in the night
Those eternal promises
'come to us, come to us'
Will forever be a mantra?

For those who are trapped
Within their own minds.

AFTER DINNER
Outspoken St. Monk

A schizophrenic who sent death threats to the mayor

a martial artist who stabbed his classmate with a fork

and a guy who thought he was Lucifer all sitting in a room

Playing crazy 8's in a mental hospital
takes on a different kinda meaning
but that's what we did
Nate, Fortune, & I

after dinner time
we'd go to the closed-off lounge
Game after game to pass the time
and even though we were locked up
removed from our lives in the air

we still smiled and laughed
delusions and all
we still shared a connection
a wavelength we were on
somehow we intersected
like it was meant to be

we were brothers
on the same boat
removed from society
I miss those guys
and the times we spent

Nate gave me his email
for when we got out
but I never did email him
and I gave Fortune my number
but he never called me

I guess that's life and such,
hope they're doing good now
where ever they are...

WORDS OF A DAMAGED WOMAN
By Lucy Slessor

My time ended the minute I began. I may sit and watch and see all, but know that inside I am dying.

The ones who came and gave their love so freely did fail to mention the small, printed clauses that resulted in my bound heart amidst the bloodied rags amongst which it sits.

A by-product of a thing called love; a perversity of nature called trust.

And a sinful lie called hope.

But what of it? I may have died but was reborn in the haze that became my pain.

Unrestricted and driven with a gall of hateful malice and bitter thoughts that would bury themselves like worms inside my muddled and muddied brain.

Deep within those dark, moist cavities. Turning and writhing and pushing deeper forever more.

So, what of those worms? So, what of those rags?

So what?

Instead, now I sit alert and ever watchful of the ties that bind me to this hateful planet, littered with sadism and malevolence.

Like a spider in its web of silks, nestled deep in the bosom of temptation, I sit and watch and wait.

Wait, that is, until the strike offers itself up to me.

Those poor, poor souls. What of them? Bloodied and bruised by the trials and tribulations of wearing a human skin. Carrying a human heart. Heavy with the burden of a human soul.

How they will oft look up to see me but are instead met by the mask that best pleases them.

I should pity them, really; their sad, little lives driven by ego and the desire to become their own god.

Little ants.

Little ants scurrying through the undergrowth, barely pausing to take word or see what lies in front of them, beside them, or under them.

But, I see. I choose to look. I choose to burn their brain with my words, scorch their skin with my touch, and brand their heart and soul to me forever.

Let my words seduce you; let them play with you. You ask for it not, but I shall take it. Because I choose to. Because I want them.

The more you deny me, I shall move forward, and you shall stay waiting for me to take that pain and replace it with my own.

And in my pain, you shall revel; you shall writhe in a blend of agony and ecstasy, unable to think anything outside of that pain.

You will ache for my words, the tender touch of a single finger brushed against your arm, so electrifying that it causes each hair to stand on end and a perpetual tingle to your skin.

My mark will be left within you, penetrating deep inside, creating a hunger that none other than I can sate.

You will want that pain so badly and so maddeningly that it will be with you every single minute of the day and every second of the night.

You will start to see through mine own eyes a life you never knew existed before, for with the curse comes also the blessing,

A devil and angel that walk in-hand with one other.

And therein lies the rub.

For the prize contains its imprint, and that imprint will carry with it a thousand-fold tears and cries of desperation. One cannot appreciate the blessing without the pain that partners it.

An irony of satirical humour that holds you in its rapturous embrace, both applauding you and laughing at you in one split second of perpetually looped time.

You will yearn for it. And I shall cry for you.

But my tears will not last, nor will they be allowed to dry by themselves.

I understand my being now. I understand my gift.

I am mistress to the art of pain.

MANIA

By Peter Hickman

Butterflies fluttering
Deep within your downward depths
Pitiful pangs of pain
With every shallow breath
Muscle malnutrition
Brought on by the aches
And moans of a body
Which has had all that it can take

DO NOT HATE ME FOR MY TEARS

By Helen Smith

do not hate me for my tears
understand
I have healing to do
I have wounds
I am broken
there are cracks where I need to be strong
but this is not all
I will ever be
you have seen the darkest
fears and pain and ugly scars
do not judge me on these things alone
I am more than my damaged parts
one day the scars will be
so small
I will not have to fight
and hide and cry
please
don't hate me for my failures
love me for what you know I can be
what I know I will be
hold me while I weep and
let me be strong in your embrace
your love, your faith will help me
heal myself
I don't ask you to
hold me up, but help me find the
strength I have to hold myself
to hold your hand
and let me hold you when you're falling

trust in me
my love for you
together we are better
than the sum of our parts
understand
I am hurting
I don't mean to hurt you
understand
I am trying
I am doing the best I can
because nothing matters more
and sometimes I will fail
sometimes I will bleed and cry
but please
do not hate me
I am only human
I have healing to do
and I am trying
I am trying
I am trying

A LAST LETTER TO THE WORLD
(A POEM ABOUT DEPRESSION)

By Jackie Chou

You have been to me a tease
etching little scars
all over my exterior

What a ghastly sight
to be medicated, healed
day after day

only to have the wounds
opened again
the therapy undone

So I beg you
to go deeper
kill the fleshy part of my heart

My love, do not be wishy-washy
do not stop what you do
at the sight of my tears

It only leaves me lying awake
night after night
paralyzed by my grief

Take my hand
and lead me to the knife, the pills
to a sensible way to die

I am tired
of another night
sitting with the pain

Make me the martyr of my life
though I know it is worth
more than I think

The weight of it all
obliterates
my fragile will to survive

MY DEMONS

By Jon Orrell

Mental illness,
A stigma or a title nobody wants,
Why? We are all human; we all suffer similar experiences,
So why do we not talk?

I'm guilty of this,
five years ago I was paralysed.
It took me four years and ten months to talk.
It gripped me.
How can I explain to family and friends
I can't feel pain in my right side?
I can't feel hot or cold either.
I should be able to talk; they care and love for me.

But still, I don't talk? Why?
To look at me, people would never know.
I smile my way through life,
Hiding behind my poker face.
I don't come from a broken home.
I've never not had a hot meal on the table.
I'm loved, I am cared for.
For most, that's all they see,
It's all I'm prepared to show.
That's probably why my demons grow.

Not talking has caused mental health problems.
I have self-harmed once,
Not to end and nor for a cry of help,
But simply to feel different

To let a new emotion in my body,
To see if I can feel.
That's probably why my demons grow.

Yet I still don't talk?
I needed someone to ask about it.
Recognise it.
Be blunt about it.
Ask me if I'm okay,
If there's anything they can do.

Simple questions have massive impacts.
Look out for your fellow human,
But worry about the happy, funny comedian types.
Like me, they often hide.
Ask them a simple question,
You never know the impact it has.

Talk, share, and ask,
And one day this stigma will be broken.

BATTLE OF A LONE WARRIOR
Leanne Brown

Thoughts rumbling through my brain like an oncoming train,
Or a clap of thunder that rolls in from a distance.

Ringing in my ears which resonates Diomedes' piercing cry.
All the while Silence's relentless embrace encompasses my soul.

My heavy breathing whistling through my grinding teeth.

My imprisoned heart trying to escape from my chest.

Lips beginning to crack as moisture evaporates from my mouth.
Hands desperately fumbling to grab and hold something... someone.

Failing that, skin stabbed and slashed from nails through palms.
War wounds steadying the rising panic that charges through my veins.

All one can do is stare widely into nothingness.

There is no escaping from my body, no retreating from my mind, no
running from myself.

It's like falling and floating,
Like seeing nothing and then seeing everything,
Like a surge of energy and then an onerous tiredness,
Like holding your breath while gasping for air.

Fighting every day.

Missing the light, the colour and the beauty of being alive.

Missing the feeling of peace, positivity and contentment.
Missing myself.

Fighting every moment,
An internal conflict,
An ongoing battle.

I will fight. I will defeat. I will win.

I am a warrior.

THE 'A' BOMB

Lee Evans

i'm sorry
is this tea not mine?
and i don't take sugar
but two spoonfuls tastes fine

i'm sorry
i forget your name
you're my daughter? my wife?
you smell just the same

i'm sorry
that i'm missing a piece
i didn't quite hear you
was that something about release?

i'm sorry
i've gotten lost again
and knowing where i am
is now proving quite the strain

i'm sorry
but for what, i'm not sure
it just seems next to normal
when your recall is so poor

i'm sorry
i'm still in here somewhere
but with this rare clarity
i know i'm past repair

i'm sorry
am i doing something wrong?
is that why you're crying
and why you cry for so long?

i'm sorry
i really don't know your name
i can't remember
shame...

ME

By Jisha viswanathan

Me
The difference of me
You can never
Or you may not understand
The blurred visions
How i can explain
The words failing
The pillars falling
Support is sinking
Everything is crumbling
One side i sense
The pain, The anxiety
Other side i am in peace with it
Why i am not fighting it
Who is stopping me
What is that holding me
The deeper i go
It's dark, full of haze
So eerie is silence
Something in me pushing me to go
Where it is leading
No sign board on road
The unknown is soothing me
No destination, Nothing
A peace befalling

Me
The difference of me
You can never

Or you may not understand
The blurred visions
How i can explain
The words failing
The pillars falling
Support is sinking
Everything is crumbling
One side i sense
The pain, The anxiety
Other side i am in peace with it
Why i am not fighting it
Who is stopping me
What is that holding me
The deeper i go
It's dark, full of haze
So eerie is silence
Something in me pushing me to go
Where it is leading
No sign board on road
The unknown is soothing me
No destination, Nothing
A peace befalling

SILENT SYMPHONY

By Shakunthala Preeth

It's ok if everything's gone silent
Dance to the tune of your heart.

It's ok if your dreams are chained
Fly high and liberate your soul.

It's ok if you can't let it go
No one can, just hold it in.

It's ok if your words go unheard
Let your gracious moves speak volumes.

It's ok if you feel lost
We all are, trust your journey...

To this day you'll look back
And smile for not having given up.

KEEPER OF MY THOUGHTS

Jessica Macaluso

I've failed so many times
I've become use to this
I know my limits
I've planted them well
A moat created deep from within
Guarded by a force spiteful and mean
I've tried my best
But- she sneers, "You're not like the rest; your best is weak, you can't succeed!"
She's the keeper of my thoughts
She stays alert
She makes sure
She's heard
She won't be abandoned
I won't leave her behind
I'll listen to her cries
She knows better
Then to let me try
She's strong
Not fragile
It's fine
Staying With her
Here in the dark
She doesn't shut up
Not ever
She doesn't shut up
She runs constant
Her words like acid
Burning my mind

I want to cut her out
Of my head
I'll pick and
I'll claw
I'll scratch
Her voice is turned down
With each new scar that I dig
Girl interrupted from the opportunities life brings
A quitter
A loser
The little girl chants
It's the echo that reminds me
That my best
Is too weak.

SAFE?

By Carol Alena Aronoff

He wouldn't tell the orderly
in faded green scrubs
that the wooden door
enclosing him was a river,
its grain flowing in rough
waves towards him.
Nor would he say
that the walls were glowing
purple embers blowing
like feathers out the barred
window. That the vinyl floor
was burning.

The orderly with cat's claws
told him he'd feel safer inside
this tiny cell of a room.
They wanted him to be
a willing flower, open softly.
Didn't want him to attack them
or harm himself. Tightly curled,
knees to chest, on narrow bed,
he made himself the smallest target,
held his breath. Here he was safe
from demons in the day room–maybe,
but what about the NSA?

HOOKS

By Maura Coyne

Dear Anyone,

...Who Has Ever Been Harmed by Words.

This is for you.

It happens.

Maybe you have already risen above, or maybe you are on your way, but don't quit. Take those words and let them flow through the chambers of your blood-soaked heart, purified, belonging to you now.

This is for Anyone who has ever forgotten who they are, been told that words don't matter, been told that they were not enough, too little, too sensitive, too much of a rebel, too lost to help themselves, too out of control.

It is even for Anyone who has used words to hurt others. Haven't we all?

Words hurt, but most importantly, words heal.

Start saying a few to yourself about your immensity, your grandeur, your messy-strong self.

Mix up your own personal batch of word potion with a side of lavender and daisy petals, and do a shot.

Treat the wounds.

Love,
You.

I do.

THE MOTH EFFECT
Robin Rich

A boy. A street light, and its orange glow pushing through windows and onto doors in their frames. The light is dressing the time of the day. This is oblivious to the wheel turning slowly inside the lamppost, visited twice a year by the man with the key to its time. One slip of his finger, and that light will be at odds with the solar system.

I do not think he cares.

The boy is at odds with time and is himself behind some kind of grey door.

The lamplighter—let's call him Ed—is wrack-headed over the outsourcing of street utilities to the private sector. Long letters over pensions; Transfer and Protection of Employment. The union meetings and threat of strikes have interfered with the quality of his time twiddling.

So, on the street with the boy outside, one lamp had its time, and the rest sort of fit in with the drifting sun-rise-set.

Jump to Brit: summer time.

Yet in lamp-time the orange glow made its shape in the dark a flickering beacon. Ed twisted knobs; no swapping bulbs allowed. The crack of electricity a buzz in the Argon, and the air filing in with the gentle tick of the grey wheel behind the dirty door near the boy's ear. The sound moved, and the ultrasonic played above him with bat and moths drawn into the sphere of light that, a blink away from the sodium bulb, was grey shades stained brown.

The detail was in the sounds and minds making a world in the lamp-time.

Is the universe round? Yes, in lamp-time. The grey-brown stain ended at nothing, and creatures appeared in it to orbit the focus and swirl like dirty water down a hole. But in this case, sort of up in the hole. The fire in the sky, a flash of life in a rush, other than the boy who, for all worlds, was the haste and pallor of a window dummy.

He stood in pyjamas on the edge of the stain in tartan slippers . A towel away from a Linus/Ford Prefect dressing up. A hormone's drift away from a Wilde dressing gown. His neck pushing hair down his nape and humming—between mimics of diving planes and ack-ack fire—the Dam Buster March. Eyes blinking the raster in impossible colours for 1943, the dogfights and burning tail spins of aeroplanes rippling the screen. All the time, the incessant tick of the grey wheel, locked in by Ed, counted down the end of the Universe.

Behind him, a crack of blue light was filled by a Mother's shout.

"Luke!" She turn and quieter behind her

"Help Dad. He's off on one. Again."

Louder, "Luke!. Luke! . Get back to bed now!"

In lamp-time, the Lancasters morphed into many Millennium Falcons and, the Fokkers into Tie Fighters. The thud of machine-gun fire was suddenly a high pitched squeal from the boy Luke of lasers and the song a fluid and synthetic beep of John Williams. The hysteria made cables of his neck, and in the break between film cells and projector gates and... hope.

"Use the Force... Let go!" played out in the locked down lamp-time . Guidance systems pushed to one side and filled with blue-lit, zoomed-in reality, and with her drink sour breath.

"Look. Look . Luke, they are just dead moths."

An Advanced Tie fighter with his Dad in it did not spin off into safety.

Luke screamed.

He could not bear their little deaths.

"WRAITHS"

Moriah

I see girls
aged 11-17
Not in a grave but already rotting.

I see girls
who aren't real girls
empty inside,
the dead men walking.

Sometimes the waking world can't tell because they're blinded by the
illusion that faking it creates.

They can't tell that they walk among us like wraiths,
but I know.

I know because I was one too,
with the life drained from my eyes and the weight of pounds lost
that I was still carrying.

It's incredible how they carry on.

Incredible because even now I fail to understand how the suffering
that was so potent
could not be felt or tasted by the world around me.

The appearance of normal.

And yet, behind the walls, holding these human souls, are the very
fires of hell, consuming.

So they continue walking
neither living nor dead
at the bottom of the ninth of their bare minimum lives
barely scraping by
no extra innings for the players of this game.

They want to leave early.

Sometimes I want to return to their ranks
the skeleton crew with the sunken-in eyes
and bodies that will expire before their time.

But therein the victory lies
there's too much color in the pages of my life
to make me return to the bleached black and white.

THE BLACK OCTOPUS

By Chris Connolly

There has been a struggle lately
Upstairs
with the black octopus,
its million tentacles
and anthracitic ink
purpling pristine waters.

Each moment elongates
Upstairs
with the black octopus
clinging to the ceiling
to the walls
to the insides of my home.

It arrived flinging shingles from their rivets
rattling windows without warning
its shape a screaming shadow;
it squirmed itself inside
and settled in up there
as if for winter.

The black octopus rages now
Upstairs
turning walls white to black
furniture back to front
yanking sparking wires from sockets
and insisting that I watch.

Who knows how long it will be
Upstairs
before the shadow yields and light is let return:
the black octopus
unlike most guests
cannot simply be asked to leave.

SCARS

By: Nancy Xiong

I know how you feel
You wish it wasn't real
'Cause every time that you open your eyes
You die a little more inside
Bang, bang

Chorus:
Open up the door
'Cause baby they want more
They'll never stop looking for you
So baby, go ahead do what you got to do
Find your way through the dark
Baby, make your mark
If you can stop the blood from falling in vain
Just don't let them realize
That they're breaking your heart

He doesn't want me to share
But somehow he really thinks he cares
That's when he told me that I need to stop
'Cause love isn't fair
Bang, bang

Chorus:
Open up the door
'Cause baby they want more
They'll never stop looking for you
So baby, go ahead do what you got to do
Find your way through the dark

Baby, make your mark
If you can stop the blood from falling in vain
Just don't let them realize
That they're breaking your heart

BEFORE THERE WERE PILLS

By Carol Alena Aronoff

Alone on a gray steel bed in a gray
room with no window except in the door,
they said she was a danger to herself.

Postpartum, they called her. Blue,
down, melancholy–words too shallow
to reach her ghost dance.

Only a shell remained, a brittle husk waiting
for nothing. Electroshock would snap her
out of it, doctors decided–without asking.

They wanted me to watch. To see her struck
by lightning, jolted to her core. Tied to a gurney,
twitching, flopping around like a dying fish.

A dying I could never forget. A death
of the spirit while the body still lived.

Memories gone, personality all but erased.
Docile as a feather with no wind, she sat
and waited for the spark to return.

SUICIDAL TENDENCIES

By Peter Hickman

Like a chocolate egg that's bought at Easter,
I'm merely a hollow shell;
A wounded person so incomplete
That when I try to smile, it's to no avail.

Just like a pervert's mind, mine's wandering;
It fixates in the same way,
Although the subtext is different
As it's myself I'd like to lay.

That's right, I've got suicidal tendencies;
Thoughts that often come and go,
But you wouldn't see it on my face
As it's been etched beneath my so solemn glow.

A glow which, as such, is devoid of colour
And thus, shaded black and white;
A shade, I fear, when at its peak
Will possess me to extinguish my own light.

SHIFTING POLARITIES

By Lindsey Woodward

I sing the body electric
For it is high voltage energy coursing through my every cell
No separation between soul and flesh

I find myself adorned with flamboyant impenetrable cape
Newfound ability to fly
To leap over buildings unaware that I could topple

The fall's inevitability an un-germinated seed
These somnambulist feet have forgotten what the ground feels like
Forgotten that it ever existed

I soar through cosmic reveries
Orating in technicolour hues
My eyes never before so bright see a timeless masterpiece

While the rest of the world turns and tosses out the sopping abstraction
Of finger-painted oils permeated with illusion
There is no calm following this wretched storm

They call me a hurricane
This time, they are right.
I hide in layered slumberous veils
Buried beneath torrent drenched soil

I am not manure
Manure promotes growth

I am base. I am shit.

My laughter that once echoed through hallways and streets
Once ardently beat eardrums and hearts
Is scratched vinyl in a lonesome roadside cardboard box

Abandoned and discarded from memory
I will sleep until dawn's sacred sun
Pokes its forlorn head above a forgotten horizon

I will sleep until beckoned by a languid smile
Inviting me back
To the world of the living

"EAGLES"

Moriah

Sometimes,
Every few days at least,
I fall and don't know how to get back up.

A verse given to me tells me I will rise up like with wings like eagles.

Yet I am so low to the ground
And I am so lonely
I see my problems before me,
Within me,
As if they have become me.

I know I can exist without them,
But they are so stitched into the fibers of me,
Woven throughout my skin.

Maybe that's why I tried to cut them out.
I failed. The problems are still there.

Now scars are too.

I want to scream.
I want to laugh and cry.

All at once, I feel them all stirring inside me. Bubbling up, threatening to erupt in the form of little choked halfway giggles—halfway whimpers and forceful exhalations.

I get on my bike and go on a ride.

I'm stuck at a crosswalk, a light that won't change
And it awakens that anger in me
As a familiar voice sings in my headphones

Rise up, rise up
With wings like eagles...

I curse.
I rant out loud as I roll along empty roads.
I complain and ask impossible questions.

Why me?

I shouldn't feel like this. I know it. I announce it.
I tell myself and anyone listening that no one deserves this kind of life.

I crank as fast as possible up a hill until I feel like my lungs will burst, letting the anger drive me.

I swear out loud, with my headphones blaring in my ears, that I will do anything to prevent this happening to others.
I say that everyone living with this, I wish I could take it away from them.

Then I crest the hill and let myself roll down the other side,
gaining speed,
and I don't try to stop it.

I put my arms out and fly,
And I rise up with wings like eagles.

Printed in Great Britain
by Amazon